RISK-FREE

ADVERTISING

WILEY SERIES ON MARKETING MANAGEMENT

Series Editor: **FREDERICK E. WEBSTER, Jr.**
The Amos Tuck School
of Business Administration
Dartmouth College

GEORGE S. DOMINGUEZ, *Marketing in a Regulated Environment*
ROBERT D. ROSS, *The Management of Public Relations: Analysis and Planning External Relations*
VICTOR WADEMAN, *Risk-Free Advertising: How to Come Close to It*

Risk-free Advertising

How to Come Close to It

VICTOR WADEMAN
Victor Wademan & Company

A WILEY-INTERSCIENCE PUBLICATION

JOHN WILEY & SONS, New York • London • Sydney • Toronto

Library of Congress Cataloging in Publication Data:

Wademan, Victor, 1939
    Risk-free advertising.

    (Wiley series on marketing management)
    "A Wiley-Interscience publication."
    1. Advertising.   2.   Advertising management.
I.   Title.

HF5821.W25   659.1   77-8083
ISBN 0-471-02714-6

Printed in the United States

10 9 8 7 6 5 4 3 2

To

Mary, Isabel, and Margaret

with love

And to my parents

with admiration

Series Editor's Foreword

Marketing management is among the most dynamic of the business functions. On the one hand it reflects the everchanging marketplace and the constant evolution of customer preferences and buying habits, and of competition. On the other hand, it grows continually in sophistication and complexity as developments in management science are applied to the work of the marketing manager. If he or she is to be a true management professional, the marketing person must stay informed about these developments.

The Wiley Series on Marketing Management has been developed to serve this need. The books in the series have been written for managers. They combine a concern for management application with an appreciation for the relevance of developments in such areas of management science as behavioral science, financial analysis, and mathematical modeling, as well as the insights gained from analyzing successful experience in the marketplace. The Wiley Series on Marketing Management is thus intended to communicate the state-of-the-art in marketing to managers.

Virtually all areas of marketing management will be explored in the series. Books now available or being planned cover advertising management, industrial marketing research, brand loyalty, sales management, product policy and planning, public relations, overall marketing strategy, and financial aspects of marketing management. It is hoped that the series will have some effect in raising the standards of applied marketing management.

FREDERICK E. WEBSTER, JR.

Hanover, New Hampshire
June 1977

Preface

Just before the turn of the century John Wanamaker, America's first modern advertiser, both in size of budget and professionalism of technique, is reported to have said, "Half my advertising is wasted. The trouble is, I can't tell which half."

Yet even now, eight decades later, advertisers still tend to wring their hands over advertising as a "black box" operation. Costly, arcane in its development, and seemingly unmeasurable.

Which is not to say that, in the interim, consistent and intelligent attempts have not been made by its practitioners to add a measure of predictability to advertising. Since the publication of Claude Hopkins' *Scientific Advertising* in 1923, for example, a string of excellent books on how to produce better advertising has been written by admen.

Most of these books—including *How To Write A Good Advertisement, Macy's, Gimbel's, and Me, Confessions Of An Advertising Man,* and *Reality In Advertising*—have concentrated on how to create advertising, however, rather than on how to manage it. As a result, the advertising client has not received anywhere near as much practical pedagogy on how to increase his contribution to the advertising process as has the advertising agent.

The purpose of this book is to bring a small measure of balance to that equation. And, given its emphasis on techniques for reducing the *risk* inherent in advertising, it is especially intended not only for advertising professionals, but also for those nonadvertising managers—presidents, treasurers, controllers, manufacturing executives—whose real role in shaping the character of their company (and therefore its effective advertisability) has long been neglected.

This, then, is a book about how to manage advertising, looked at from the client side. As a product of a working adman's experience, it is also a book about what gets results in advertising, not what comes in a textbook.

In this respect, it aims to tell you not what will result in no risk in advertising, but what will result in less risk. Acceptable risk. Investment grade rather than speculative risk.

VICTOR WADEMAN

New York
June 1977

Contents

RISK-FREE

ADVERTISING

ONE

THE HOLY GRAIL OF
Measurability

More than any other function in business, advertising encourages the search for a Holy Grail. The Holy Grail of measurability.

There are several reasons for this. First, there is advertising's basic characteristic as a non–balance sheet investment. For, in an accounting sense, advertising is a noncapitalized intangible that does not linger long for all to see under "Assets," but quickly wreaks its positive or negative effect right on the bottom line. (Which, to anyone who holds responsibility for authorizing significant advertising funds, is as frightening in fact as it is in theory.)

Advertising also does not lend itself to DCF, present value, or any of the other sophisticated forms of cash flow analysis, since its "flows" simply are not that estimable.

And finally, let's be realistic. The measurement of advertising's results—at a time when enormous consumer, economic, and organizational change leads the American businessman to an all-time peak interest in those results—still is a very imprecise process, and, some would argue, not measurable at all.

Ask yourself, for example, what kind of goals you can legitimately set for your advertising.

Profit? Very, very difficult. A moment's reflection will suggest there are normally too many variables other than advertising that normally affect profits. Changes in product ingredient costs, processing costs, physical distribution costs, and a laundry list of other expenses, as well as changes in pricing, competitive activity, or the performance/service benefits you offer, can individually or collectively hide the profit or loss impact of an advertising campaign, whether it's remarkably successful or remarkably bad.

Sales? Maybe. But again, such measurement can be twisted grotesquely by other factors in your marketing mix, including some of those just mentioned. When all is said and done, in fact, advertising's results in sales remains a yardstick best measured in controlled test markets rather than full-scale expansion situations.

Memorability testing of your new campaign or longer-term consumer awareness of your advertising? Well, probably the greatest advances of all have been made in measuring both the short and long-term communication power of advertising, and it is correct to argue that the correlation between advertising memorability and sales effectiveness is high. But try selling a Starch score to your Board of Directors if sales and profits are off target.

Lack of advertising measurability does not accrue from a want of trying, however. In fact, the measurement of advertising effectiveness has been the subject of such a hotbed of marketing science in recent years, that nonadvertising executives would laugh if you tried to apply some of the same techniques to their functions.

In pursuit of advertising's effectiveness marketing scientists have, for example, literally dilated pupils, stared at women's buying behavior from behind one-way glass, interviewed shoppers till their clipboards sagged in exhaustion, run out least-squares till Hell won't have it, Starched, Galluped, and Nielsened, employed canonical correlations, thematic apperception, short-termed damped oscillation prior to stabilization, Koyck's model of distributed lags, and both backward and forward elimination of irrelevant variables.

About the only thing they have not done is shoot consumers full of scopolamine. Or have they?

One wag even devised the following model ". . . for the *simplified* budgeting of advertising."

Exhibit 1.1 A simplified mathematical model for budgeting advertising

$$_{,t} = rs_{i,t-1} + (1-r) \left[b \, \frac{Q_i \, (P_{i,t})^{-\epsilon_p}}{\sum\limits_{j=1}^{n} Q_j \, (P_{j,t})^{-\epsilon_p}} + (1-b) \, \frac{Q_i \, (P_{i,t})^{-\epsilon_p} (A_{i,t})^{\epsilon_A}}{\sum\limits_{i=1}^{n} Q_j \, (P_{j,t})^{-\epsilon_p} (A_{j,t})^{\epsilon_A}} \right] + \epsilon_{1,t} \,(1)$$

Only seven men are said to be capable of deciphering it. Unfortunately, none work on Madison Avenue.

So the problem remains. When it comes to measuring advertising, regression analysis, where is thy sting?

Lest you as an advertising client feel frustrated in your desire to put your finger on what you're getting for your money, however, consider the lilies of the field. Your ad agency personnel, and the feebleness of the two major kinds of research from which they are supposed to produce the brilliant advertising you so ardently, and legitimately, desire.

Demographic data, for instance, tell them things like your customer's age, sex, income, education, home ownership, and number of roller skates possessed. All of which is usable enough in some ways, as we will see later. But as a creator of advertising, just exactly what do you *say* to this skeleton?

The even newer "science" of psychographics is, admittedly, designed to bridge the gap between the bare-boned demographic statistic and the flesh and blood human being whom your copywriter must captivate. But here, as a revealing example of the utility of this technique, are some of the intricate, irrelevant, and even contradictory psychological characteristics of that mundane creature, the electric drill buyer, as given by the leading syndicated (and therefore affordable) research service in the psychographic field:

He is affectionate, awkward, egocentric, refined, tense, eco-
logically minded, brave, kind, cautious and domineering.

Quite a guy. Although most copywriters probably had no
notion the home workshopper was so complicated.

At any rate, as a result of Madison Avenue's continuing
overemphasis on purely laboratory approaches such as these
to take the risk out of advertising, there has even grown up
among some more practical minds (including those of clients
interested in making money) the reactionary but understand-
able viewpoint that while facts are important in advertising,
intuition is even more important.

Which is partially true. The problem is, you have to be
careful not to throw the baby out with the washwater.

For the point of all the foregoing was not to knock the
dedicated researcher, but simply to remind the reader that the
infallible technique for measuring then motivating the human
heart does not yet exist; is not likely to exist; or if it did exist,
it would almost certainly cost too much. And that in advertising, as in any other area of business, the value of perfect information, even if available, would probably not be worth the
cost.

However, the discarding of a *fact*-based approach to your
advertising is at least as wrong, and far more mischevious, than
relying solely on laboratory-type research to take the risk out
of it.

As a matter of fact, the whole premise of this book is that
there does exist a sufficient base of practical *business* information, and sensible ways to process that information, for you to
take an approach to advertising that qualifies as investment
grade, as opposed to speculative. *From the outset, however,
you must realize that it involves a more demanding, participa-
tive, and involved role in the generation of your firm's advertising by all the members of your management team, than you
had perhaps expected.*

Will it be worth it?

Is the payout of your advertising worth it?

And perhaps we ought to lay one myth to rest right here, because clearly, advertising *does* pay out. The cynics about this having been put on the defensive a few years ago by the findings of the ground-breaking John Morrill study.

Published jointly by the *Harvard Business Review* and by the McGraw-Hill Company, this study, comprising over 100,000 personal interviews covering some 1000 industrial companies in 90-odd end-use markets, reported the following:

- *Given adequate frequency, most advertising is extremely profitable.* The total cost of selling to customer groups consistently exposed to advertising does, in fact, drop 10 to 30%.
- *There are few markets in which advertising is not profitable.* This includes situations in which sales coverage is already intense; where sales are primarily negotiated by top management; and even where product differences are small and great emphasis is put on price to make the sale.
- *The nonadvertiser stands at a serious disadvantage in any well-advertised market.* His cost of selling to customer groups exposed to his competitor's advertising may actually increase 20 to 40%.

The problem, therefore, is not that advertising is an inherent speculation that typically fails to pay for itself. The problem is to make advertising the most effective investment you can. One to which your whole management team will feel committed, because they have developed its rationale. And one about whose achievements they will ultimately feel proud, because they have managed it before the fact, not just measured it afterward.

TWO

THE PRECONDITIONS TO

Money Making Advertising

It may occur to you that, in placing greater emphasis on managing rather than measuring advertising, I am also implying that a double standard is frequently applied to advertising. That management all too frequently asks advertising to justify itself on a scientific basis, without applying that same yardstick to the rest of its capital deployment or management processes.

But, even recognizing the huge size of some advertising budgets, asking advertising to be scientific is about as reasonable as asking business in general to be scientific. Both exist to make money in the marketplace, not prove something in a test tube.

Yet if this is true, then logic and the shortcomings of the current managerial methods used to develop advertising suggest a very important point. That *the next major improvement in advertising accountability will likely come not from the agency research department but from the client side of adver-*

tising. And that the best prospect for that improvement lies in a broad-scale revolution in client advertising management style.

Which I believe might profitably take two forms. First, acceptance of the principle that *targeted digging for relevant business facts in constructing an ad program is better than reliance upon abstruse research*. That the key to success in advertising (just like the key to success in business in general) is attention to fundamentals, not sophisticated measurement techniques. And second, that *a structured approach to the development of a total corporate strategy is an absolute precondition to the development of a money-making advertising strategy*. In effect, that payout advertising proceeds from a total business—not just an old-fashioned marketing—plan.

The first of these points raises the key question, however, "Is an effective and practical fact base for increasing the payout potential of advertising really available?" (After all, I've just finished arguing that definitive techniques for measuring advertising's after-the-fact results, aren't.)

The answer, I believe, is, "Yes." But again, only assuming company management is willing to replace the limited, descriptive issue of, "How did we do with our advertising?" with the more productive, "What if we followed this particular advertising strategy?. . ." That is, *if they concentrate on out-front, before-the-fact strategic planning to increase advertising's impact and to reduce the judgmental errors often associated with it, rather than on research that merely tries to measure what's right or wrong after the horse is out of the stable*.

That the information necessary to run a strategic-minded advertising system really does exist is most apparent, I think, in companies of any size and modern financial method. For highly valuable strategic planning tools like product profit contributions, fixed and variable cost designations, costs by market, and so forth, can all normally be kicked out by a company's financial control system, if it has any control system at all.

I would also argue that the market data needed to manage advertising strategically is usually available or buyable as well—for example, data on actual usage of a product (such as consumer usage habits and usage frequency); data on the movement of the product out through available distribution channels (including share by market, condition of the inventory pipeline, and the effect of specific promotions on distribution); plus media information (coverage, efficiency, and audience measurement). Unlike guessing about advertising's results, strategic thinking about advertising doesn't have to be a garbage in–garbage out proposition, therefore.

Even with the availabiilty of the information needed to make a switch to strategic advertising possible, however, such a change in advertising management emphasis is not easy for many firms. For underlying it is the serious question of whether a company is really a sales or profit-minded operation.

That is, experience strongly suggests that a company will never persevere in the hard job of trading formularized answers for the structured analysis of its investments (including advertising), unless its whole executive team is committed to making money. Nor do I think it will surprise the reader to say not all companies are. Volume, particularly, dazzles many managers, with the consequence that sales become paramount and marketing (or disciplined efforts at making money from sales) an afterthought.

Thus the approach to getting better results from advertising that I detail in this book may be a more stringent and time-consuming undertaking than some companies are prepared to bite off. Principally because it demands going beyond a knowledge of the market niches your company might occupy (the so-called "positioning" approach), to a knowledge of the real fit of your firm to its market. In terms of your underlying corporate objectives, your controlling profit economics, and, in fact, all the human, organizational, and financial resources that define your company's real ability to essay a given advertising strategy profitably.

When all is said and done, however, I feel this more demanding approach to shaping advertising investment will give intelligent, logical, and truthful corporate communication its due, at last, as a motivating force. (A particularly important development, I think, in these days when that old postwar consumer standby, the status seeker, is increasingly evolving into that new and better human being, the truth seeker. Who is, however, a country mile harder to sell.)

I also believe the approach to advertising I outline is one that will interest the imaginative manager, because it suggests that the basic philosophy and drive of an organization (which a manager can create) have far more to do with successful advertising than the purely monetary resources his firm may or may not possess.

Finally, by its emphasis on the interfunctional coordination that is needed in advertising strategy development and execution, the approach I advocate (and this is important) also suggests that successful advertising strategy is not so much a hard-to-find inspiration, but a readily achievable distillation. That the Big Idea you've been looking for in advertising—the one that always pays out—is really findable. Because the Big Idea is you.

THREE

THE IMPORTANCE OF YOUR
Corporate
Objectives

There is an axiom in advertising, "The more you tell, the more you sell."

The problem is, an advertising agency can never really tell a company's story in depth until management first defines it for them in depth. Possibly the greatest single mistake of the unsophisticated advertiser, in fact, is the error he makes of letting his agency people substitute their own purely marketing objectives for what he really wants his company or product to stand for in the market, long term.

Advertising run this way usually winds up as opportunism, not investment. For unless top management knows what kind of company or product to have, how can the creators of advertising really know what kind of ads to have?

TOP MANAGEMENT'S ROLE IN THE
ADVERTISING PROCESS

What I am suggesting here is that, to portray a winning character in its advertising, a company must first have well-defined corporate objectives.

The problem, however, is that corporate objectives often aren't stated well, and for good reason. Top management frequently doesn't work hard enough at it.

For example, here's a corporate objectives statement of a type you can distill from many annual reports you pick up:

- Achieve a 12% or greater return on the equity invested in our business.
- Strive for a 150 million dollar sales volume, becoming the leading factor in our product category.
- Finance our growth through internally generated profits.

Succinct. Definite. Hard-nosed. But not specific enough about this company's real aspirations and talents to provide a basis for serious advertising thinking.

The underlying problem is that the management of this company gives no evidence of embracing the so-called marketing concept. That is, the approach whereby top management, to achieve sound promotional programs for their company, provides specific guidelines to operating management for the committing of assets to marketing activities such as advertising; clearly defines which products and markets are fair game for such investment; then sees that a sound challenge is provided to the promotional alternatives that are developed.

Or, to put it another way, what a company needs to define the role promotional tools like advertising can productively play for it, is a package of objectives—financial, marketing, organizational. All of which must be logically integrated and each of which must, in turn, cast light on the vital issues of the risks the company is willing to bear in its promotional investments; the basic growth strategies and charters advertising is empowered to support; and how a company's whole organization will get behind its advertising claims to make the ads it runs more than "just advertising."

THE NATURE OF OBJECTIVES

It may be wise before we go further to define the term corporate objective. Put simply, I define a corporate objective as an overall end toward which a company's effort is directed. Unlike a goal, therefore, it is nonquantitative. Rather, it deals more in *the character and quality of the company you want* than the purely numerical sales or share or profitability targets you may also wish to set up.

The relative painlessness of this definition is complicated, of course, by the fact that there are so many objectives from which a company can choose; each of which will have a different impact on advertising strategy. For example, (as is common enough) a company may establish as its primary objective the displacement of a competitor as the leader in its field. And if its advertising agency takes that goal at face value, it has set up what amounts to a very competitive objective for them to achieve, which will definitely affect advertising strategy.

Given such an objective, for instance, advertising claims very likely would be geared to competitive weaknesses; advertising's "tone of voice" might well be rougher and tougher than normal; and media funds probably would be allocated toward markets or business that competition would especially like to protect, or where it is especially vulnerable.

By contrast, if a company's primary objective is a high return on investment, its advertising might well be focused against high-margin market segments; perhaps use more of a "class" tone in individual ads; and include copy that stresses the product's own benefits without reference to competition.

The more precise and well-integrated your objectives, in fact, the better your advertising people can respond to them,

or productively argue with you about them.* In short, name
your objective and you will properly receive a different advertising plan depending on what that objective is. Fail to specify
your objectives, and you can easily derail your advertising
before you even get it out in the market, because you have
deprived your advertising people of any stable basis for shaping it *strategically*.

TYPES OF CORPORATE OBJECTIVES

I said earlier that it is unlikely that a company will get consistently productive advertising unless it develops a logically
integrated package of objectives.

To make myself as clear as possible on this key point, here
is a list of potential objective-setting areas from which I believe
such a package might be chosen.

A SUGGESTED RANGE OF CORPORATE OBJECTIVES TO GUIDE ADVERTISING STRATEGY DEVELOPMENT

Financial Objectives

- Required return (involving a possible selection among
  ROA, ROE, or ROI)
- Sales
- Market share
- Earnings or earnings per share
- The inherent quality and consistency of earnings
- Debt/equity ratio
- Merger/acquisition

---

* An important corollary to this is that corporate objectives ought to
be tailored to individual products, product groups, and divisions, since
for competitive, cost, and product acceptance reasons, across-the-
board objectives are usually not realistic.

Marketing Objectives

- Relative emphasis of major growth options
- Business charters or missions of individual products or operating divisions

Organizational Objectives

- Management style and climate

Since I also believe that the rightness or wrongness of any one of these objectives for a given company can affect the payout of its advertising far more than does the brilliance of its advertising copy, the efficiency of its media plan or, even, the size of its ad budget, let's now analyze the usefulness of each of these major objectives in guiding advertising toward firm and productive ground.

Financial Objectives

Of all the objectives a company ever sets, the financial are undoubtedly the most popular. For one thing, setting them is fun.

In good measure, that's because many managers make the mistake we already mentioned of confusing objectives with goals. Instead of focusing their company's efforts on a coordinated management effort to improve return-on-assets (for example), what they all too frequently wind up with is only a constantly ascending ROA bogey.

The numerical approach to objective setting is nice in that it tends to keep bothersome questions of achievement at bay as well. The whole situation being analogous to the "long-term planning" some companies do. Page upon page of quantified goals and budgets, without any real *thinking* about the strategic issues that are likely to affect the long-term welfare of their company.

By contrast, real corporate financial objectives must, in my judgment, be supported by a careful consideration of the *risk* the company is prepared to assume to achieve those objectives. Certainly, management's taste for risk varies considerably from company to company; and when advertising is the key tool that will be relied on to achieve corporate objectives, you are per se dealing with risk.

For example, let's consider the company whose "objectives" we referred to at the start of this chapter. The one that wants a 12% ROE and a 150 million dollar sales level, all financed through internally generated profits.

Let's further suppose their actual starting position looked like Exhibit 3.1.

Exhibit 3.1   The Hope Springs Eternal company's starting sales and ROE profile

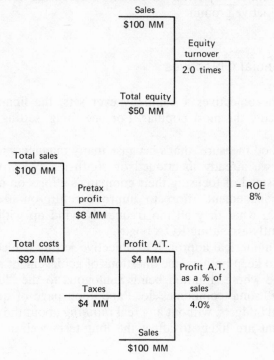

Unless margins can be improved considerably, therefore, this company literally will have to double its sales to realize its profitability objective, not just hit 150 million (Exhibit 3.2).

Exhibit 3.2   Hope Springs Eternal's sales requirement to reach its ROE goal

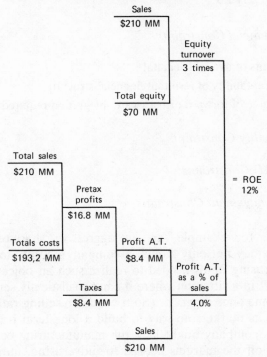

Call this sloppy staff work if you like. The point is that even a modest-sounding increase in some financial measures may require astounding increases in sales which, if taken literally as objectives, will require astounding increases in risk taking as well. The moral being: the way to approach financial objectives that keeps you from having to perform advertising miracles, is to look for the *constraints* involved in reaching your objectives.

Now, all I mean here is that no company is big enough or rich enough or smart enough to achieve all the objectives it cares to. There are always limitations to corporate resources, the principal ones being:

MAJOR CONSTRAINTS TO ACHIEVING CORPORATE OBJECTIVES

Financial Constraints

- Limits of available capital
- Acceptability of resultant financial structure
- Degree of forward or backward integration required

Facility Constraints

R&D Constraints

Management Constraints

Thus, for example, an overaggressive share-of-market objective may not only stretch a company's ability to finance the advertising funds needed to realize such an objective, but also result in a situation where it can't realistically service the new volume once it gets it. (So it winds up selling rather than servicing its market: no way to build a long-term franchise.)

Or, a company might lack the manufacturing economics to throw off the margins needed for advertising, until it first back integrates to equalize its margins with those of competition. (Having back integrated, of course, it will be sensitive to domino theory risks if primary demand for its product falls off.)

The summary point is that it's impossible to know whether the financial risks you propose to achieve through advertising are either pie-in-the-sky or far, far too modest until you first think about the character of the company you really want, and the range of resources you have to get it with.

Marketing Objectives

Compared with financial objectives that tend to spawn quantified goals, marketing objectives are very process related. That's because marketing, by nature, is more of a focus than a function, and developing a clear vision of the markets they really want to be in, and the customers they want to serve, is the very essence of corporate management's marketing task.

Moreover, there is a definite chain of logic necessary to lead from corporate marketing objectives to successful product marketing objectives. This can probably be best explained by an example.

HOW THE XYZ SPORTING GOODS AND CHILDREN'S FURNITURE COMPANY'S CORPORATE MARKETING OBJECTIVES LEAD INTO REINFORCING PRODUCT MARKETING OBJECTIVES

Corporate Marketing Objective:	Increase corporate dollar profits and sales stability
Corporate Marketing Strategy:	Hold sales on our sporting goods line while increasing sales of higher-margin child care products
Children's Furniture Group Marketing Objective:	Increase child care product sales at current margin levels
Children's Furniture Group Marketing Strategy:	Increase advertising awareness of the "Childcraft" line of cribs, strollers, and changing tables in all major metropolitan markets, while introducing the new "Kinder Kare" line of tables and chairs in our five Eastern sales districts

As I believe is implicit in this example, the need for effective product and marketing leadership at the corporate level

should not involve a corporate president in the functional
aspects of his company's marketing. That's what a company
has marketing executives for.

Top management (in the person of your president or perhaps your Executive Committee) does need to take the lead
in two areas of marketing, however. First, *in defining the
growth paths that are acceptable to their company. And second, in setting up specific marketing charters or missions for
their product, market, or divisional organizations to follow.*

What I mean by "acceptable growth paths," is this. Basically, there are three major growth options a company can elect
to follow in its marketing, each of which normally represents
an ascending order of risk. The first of these is *operational
growth.* That is, increased market share or market penetration
among the customer groups you are already serving. (Market
share suggesting you will attempt to increase your percentage
of the market available to you in your product category; penetration suggesting you will try to extend the usage of your
product among your current customer groups.) Both are, from
an advertising point of view, probably the least risky approaches to corporate growth, assuming you still have "room
to grow" in current markets, and particularly if you have a
successful advertising campaign already going for you.

A company may, however, desire faster growth or greater
profitability than its current markets can offer, either because
of a slowdown in primary demand, or competitive conditions
within its markets. A good example is the situation that faced
the Volkswagen Corporation of America in recent years.

That is, after two decades of superb growth and brilliant
advertising (and with no diminution of the innovative qualities
of that advertising in sight), Volkswagen found itself in a
much-changed U.S. automobile market. And, apparently not
content with their limited prospects (which no advertising, no
matter how brilliant, possibly could have overcome), they
moved to the second, somewhat riskier corporate growth op-
tion, namely, *product development.* This can consist of a
whole series of possible improvements to your product or, as
in Volkswagen's case, a whole new generation of product (the

"Rabbit") as a line extension. Advertising's success in this case obviously is dependent not only on its own quality but also the quality of the product improvements made.

A third alternative for achieving corporate marketing growth characteristically involves even greater risk from an advertising standpoint. This is the alternative of *market development*, or electing to expand by finding a whole new class of customers for your product. The problem here is that, unlike the first two options, which offer you some kind of existing franchise to exploit, you have now sailed into clearly uncharted waters.

That is, not only will you have to persuade a whole new set of customers with different beliefs, attitudes, and habits, but you may have to do it while moving your product through new and untried distribution channels and, possibly, with a revised margin structure from which advertising itself is funded. When you choose this growth mode, therefore, advertising alone is very unlikely to do the trick for you.

It's especially wise if you take this latter course, therefore, to start thinking beyond your objectives to the second major job corporate management plays in marketing. That is, defining the fundamental marketing charters or powers you will grant line management to achieve your objectives.

Suppose, for example, as the newly appointed president of a multidivisional textile firm serving numerous end-use markets, you also find that you have a new but floundering division that is creating havoc with your established operations by selling fabric indiscriminately into their markets. (Thereby undercutting their prices, diluting their market identity, and raising executive temperatures to 104 degrees—Celsius).

The explanation you get from your new division may be that they desperately have to "cover" their high-cost manufacturing equipment with orders to avoid dragging down total corporate profits. But unless you find a maketing niche—or charter—for them, you may have a palace revolution on your hands.

On the basis of such things as your company's preferences for selling to certain markets, the versatility of the machinery your problem division possesses, and the profit potential of end-use areas unassigned to current divisions, you may therefore want to think long and hard about assigning your new division its own patch of earth, such as the following:

> Our new X division will serve the Missy (younger women's) coordinated sportswear manufacturers in California only, concentrating its fabric development for these manufacturers on department store price points. Fabric, styling, and coloration will also reflect the latest trends shown by major Paris ready-to-wear couturiers such as Kenzo, Jap, and Dorothée Bis, while being executed in 100% polyester.

Apart from getting you out of the pickle you're in with your established operations, note that such a charter has defined *the purpose, scope of activity and product line concept* of your new division. All of which will greatly help you advertise it.

For one thing, your charter has committed the new division to a proprietary customer (the California Missy woman), whose personality and tastes are now the province of a specific management group. What they say to her or the garment manufacturers who serve her in their advertising (and other promotional activities) ought to be based on more than just bloodless demography, therefore. If they do their job right, it will be based on first-hand customer *knowledge*. And who knows? Perhaps this knowledge may even reach a level that permits them to offer their customer some unique and enduring values that will convert your new operation from a commodity-type producer to a branded operation, which the average textile manager would give his right arm for.

Organizational Objectives

Defining realistic financial targets for a company, then spelling out specific growth paths and customer charters, aren't the whole battle in setting advertising objectives, however. For (in my experience at least), unless a company also has the will to make its advertising promises real, it is not likely to make much money from it, long term.

What I am basically saying here is that every advertiser—and the advertiser who provides a consumer service rather than a manufactured product particularly—should make sure he has a highly committed organization in hand before he puts a dime of advertising money on the line.

Now, many people in business who think of organization think only of structure. And while organizational structure can be important in developing and executing sound advertising strategy (as we discuss later) I, for one, think it is generally overrated. Rather, to realize the type of interfunctonal commitment that is at the heart of a well-managed advertising effort (including on-time service from manufacturing, effective product debugging from R & D, and the quality the customer ordered from quality control) basic management philosophy and processes are *much* more important, in my opinion.

A company's management philosophy and processes shape its executives to the real tasks at hand, after all. What *is* management philosophy anyway, except a well-communicated attitude of, "Here's the way we do things around here." And if that attitude is positive, if it strikes postures like, "It's O.K. to try to improve anything around here . . . there are no sacred cows . . . we all really do try to pull together and innovators are welcome," (no matter how "apple pie" that all sounds), then you probably have a favorable climate for both motivating your ad agency *and* building support for your promotional efforts throughout your organization.

Recognizing advertising as one of those "glamour" functions that nonadvertising executives really like to dabble in anyway, one client of mine even insists that his entire executive committee participate in a summary advertising strategy session before his company's advertising plan for a fiscal year is approved. He then ensures that this meeting is a donnybrook, with no possibility of any of his nonadvertising executives coming to the meeting without being fully prepared to discuss the implications of the proposed advertising plan on their area (in terms of product development lead times, performance feature tolerances, backup inventory investment required, etc.).

This approach does not make his executive's lives any easier. But I know it leads to totally committed service to his customers, with no possibility that copy tests, for example, will ever replace satisfied users as this company's ultimate criteria of advertising measurement.

Advertising can provide real "go power" to an organization, in other words. But not unless top management, and a company's president particularly, realize they can never delegate the creation of a productive environment for the development of advertising to someone else. Advertising, that is, provides go power to an organization; but an organization's own character, philosophy, and management style are what really provide go power to its advertising.

Summary

The company with a clearly defined set of objectives is like a ship with ballast. It has the specific customer commitments necessary to get its advertising into focus. It has created the basis for the interfunctional coordination necessary to give clout to its advertising claims. And because it has proved it can deal conceptually with risk, it has a far better chance of not only setting financial goals but also of reaching them. All of which is incredibly important in an area of business where there *are* no truly reliable after-the-fact evaluation techniques, only before-the-fact planning methods.

The advertising director and agency of the company taking these points to heart are, therefore, well set up to devise strategies consistent with what their company really wants to achieve, and can do. Or to disagree with the objectives they have been given, insofar as they can propose more realistic ones supported by cogent analysis. As we see in the next two chapters.

FOUR

PROFIT ECONOMICS.

Defining Advertising's Profit-Making Role

Normally, after receiving top management's statement of corporate objectives, the marketing director of a firm and his staff move into the development of their marketing and advertising plan for the coming fiscal year. The basic tool normally used for doing this is the so-called marketing position review (see Exhibit 4.1).

The purposes of this review are twofold. First, to provide the planner with sufficient knowledge about his market and his product's position in the market to enable him to identify the key problems and opportunities facing his company or brand. And second, to establish a common basis of understanding between the planner and his management reviewers about what needs to be done in marketing and advertising to realize corporate objectives. Management then is capable, with position-review facts laid before them, of weighing the alternatives presented, deciding on a course of action, then insuring the needed interfunction coordination to accomplish the plan.

Exhibit 4.1 Outline of a typical marketing position review

Areas of analysis	1. The market	2. Product position	3. Competitive developments	4. Review of successful and unsuccessful brand activities	5. Conclusions
	Total market sales volume and growth rate (in units and dollars)	Review of shipment performance, overall and by division, with reasons for variations	Strengths and weaknesses in total market, market segments, trends	What was activity?	Growth rate—will it continue? • Is growth due to increase in penetration (more people using) or in usage (same people using more, for different purposes, etc.)? • Which of these factors will cause future growth? • Will growth be even geographically or concentrated in underdeveloped areas?
	Major market segments with their respective sales and growth rates	Review of share performance, overall and by regions, channels of distribution and demographic groupings, with reasons for variations	Competition on seasonal, regional and demographic basis	Why did it succeed or fail?	
	Pertinent market profiles • Seasonal trends • Regional developments • Demographic patterns	Trends in profit performance	Analysis of competitive marketing programs • Product innovation and improvement • Pricing • Sales and	What conclusions can be drawn	Growth factors—what have been the major growth factors in our product category during the last 3-4 years? • Growth of established products • New products, new sizes • Private label and all others
	Consumer analysis • Household				

Areas of analysis

- penetration
- Repurchase patterns
- Consumer attitudes
- Usage patterns
- distribution
- Advertising and promotion

—

Expected future moves by competition

Have gains and losses been even or do they vary by division? If they vary, what appear to be the significant factors accounting for differences?
- Competitive products
- Spending differences
- Qualitative differences in advertising and promotion effort
  - Distribution by area or account type

—

What is our product performance position versus competition?
- "Blind" tests
- Attitudes

—

What packaging has worked for the product and what has not?

—

Net conclusions concerning problems and opportunities

In and of itself, there is not much wrong with this kind of approach. As far as it goes, it encourages a factual approach to the development of a marketing plan, which is critical to the subsequent development of a lower-risk advertising plan. It also draws attention to the consumers, marketing regions, channels of distribution, and competitive weaknesses on which advertising might concentrate, as well as examing successful, past interrelationships between advertising and other marketing tools. To be realistic, most companies would be well ahead of the game if they just went this far in their business planning.

Having participated in or directed the development of almost 50 marketing plans over the past 15 years, however, I am convinced it's not enough. For, useful as this approach is, it does not, in my opinion, come to grips with the issue that underlies the real payout potential of advertising. Namely, the profits advertising is able to generate by impacting on the basic *profit economics* of a firm.

In a serious way, therefore, the traditional method of preparing a marketing plan does not provide a sufficiently complete fact base either for allocating the financial or technological resources of a company behind advertising, or of specifying the key tasks of both advertising and nonadvertising executives in support of an ad program. And that's because it does not define *the economic role advertising ought to play in a company* in the first place.

PROFIT ECONOMICS: THE INTERFUNCTIONAL WAY TO ADVERTISING STRATEGY

If you construe my last statement to mean that a company ought to base its advertising on a total business rather than just a marketing plan, you're right.

But I mean something more too. That in any business, large or small, there invariably are a handful of factors that have a decisive effect not only on short-term profits, but also on long-term competitiveness. And that granting priority to these key factors in its management system is really the *only* way a company can ever confidently hope to achieve its corporate objectives.

The factors I'm referring to—a firm's profit economics—vary considerably from company to company, and industry to industry. Within a given company, they may also change with shifts in industry position, product preference levels, distribution methods, availability of raw materials, and the like. But at any given time they represent the things a company has got to do well to *win* in its industry.

In my opinion, therefore, advertising strategies not developed on the basis of these controlling product or corporate economics are so severely handicapped as to be risky in the extreme. Yet if this is so, then advertising can never be classified as an investment.

What's needed, therefore, is the application to the advertising strategy development process of a more penetrating set of analytical tools than those used in the time-honored marketing position review approach. Fortunately, these tools do not have to be invented; they already exist.

In the balance of this chapter, therefore, I illustrate some of these economic analyses and their reference to advertising, using an imaginary but plausible company as an example. Then, in the next chapter, I show how a more tightly structured marketing position review ("sequential analysis"), keyed to providing both economic *and* marketing data of a quantitative type to the advertising strategy development process, integrates advertising into the total business plan faster and more thoroughly than the traditional position review format is capable of doing.

McCARTHY'S NEW IMPROVED FURNITURE POLISH

Let's assume for the purpose of illustration in both this chapter and the next that we are dealing with a product called Mc-

Carthy's Furniture Polish. The sole brand of a firm that is the leader in its field, which is manufacturing such furniture polish for sale to consumers through food supermarkets.

Let's further assume that a year ago, this company introduced what they felt was a significantly improved polish to the market, under price discounting pressure from its two competitors. A new small size was also introduced at that time.

Since then, however, sales and profits have been consistently disappointing. In fact, they are way off target and getting worse. What's wrong and what can be done about it?

Sensitivity Analysis

Advertising is a high leverage function. But it is not necessarily the highest leverage function in a firm. Or the function in a business that should take preeminence in management's time and capital allocations, *if* the profit increase that can be expected from an improvement in some other area of the business is greater than that which would accrue from a proportionate improvement in advertising.

Moreover, advertising can also serve different economic roles for a company, depending on the realism of corporate objectives and the ways a company actually makes its money. (Some examples of these roles are: building volume, or emphasizing certain parts of the company's product mix, or helping to maintain satisfactory pricing on a product by building a quality reputation for it.)

For both these reasons, therefore, the relative precedence of a company's management tasks *in an economic sense* is something that should greatly concern the advertising planner. And one of the best ways to understand the real "rank order of jobs to be done" in a company (and by extension advertising's economic role within it) is through sensitivity analysis (see Exhibit 4.2).

As I believe is apparent from our exhibit, the soul of this analysis lies in measuring what effect a small and presumably doable improvement in managing the major economic aspects

Exhibit 4.2   Sensitivity analysis of McCarthy's business suggests that company profits are primarily volume and fixed cost sensitive

Factors that can be managed to improve profits	Effect on McCarthy's before tax profits of a 5% improvement* in this factor
Volume	22%
Price	10
Product mix (new small size versus standard size)	2
Unit variable costs	8
Fixed costs	14

* That is, an increase on such factors as volume, price, and mix; a cost decrease in variable and fixed charges.

of a product or company, will have on corporate profits. Hence the term sensitivity analysis: the profit sensitivity of the key economic elements of volume, price, cost, mix, and investment in a business to management-induced change. (With the analysis conducted on the basis of that percent improvement management thinks achievable; and with the profit improvement percentage that results being computed simply by adjusting the company's P&L to reflect the dollar profit increase each individual factor would produce at the percentage improvement postulated, percentaged against current corporate profits.)

In McCarthy's case, therefore, we see that their company is primarily volume and fixed cost sensitive, although price maintenance or improvement is important to them too.

Advertising would appear to have an important economic role in McCarthy company operations, therefore. In fact, a dual one. First, in helping to hustle enough product out the door so the high fixed cost structure implied in these numbers does not eat the company alive. And second, in building appreciation of the "new and improved" qualities of the McCarthy product so profit-sensitive developments such as the competitive price cutting that is going on do not ruin corporate profits. Thus, while we are really not very familiar with the McCarthy Company at this point, it seems safe to say that advertising probably can play a major factor in making money in this company.

Alternately, if the company had displayed profit sensitivity only to its variable costs, it would not be so necessary to start thinking about advertising's role at this standpoint. There would be no great fixed cost hurdle to get over, and a lesser threat to profits from competitive pricing developments would be posed. What's more, even a great ad campaign on a product experiencing fast-escalating variable costs usually is no economic boon. In such cases, management is usually well advised to get expenses under control first, or run the risk of the profits it creates "out front" immediately being brought to earth from behind.

Different economic profiles in different companies and on different products can change the hypotheses you draw about what needs to be done in advertising, therefore, and dramatically. You can also never forget to assess the *realism* of your opportunities to increase volume, change mix, improve pricing, and so on, no matter how appetizing theoretical changes in those factors appear. Sensitivity analysis does not depict what you can do, after all. Only what you get on the bottom line if you actually do it.

Nonetheless, unless you know what management action your profits are sensitive to, then find out what sensitivities you can really work on, why blindly spend money advertising? Or not advertising? Or advertising for the wrong economic reason?

Breakeven Analysis

What, you may ask, has the advertising strategist got to do with breakeven analysis? Isn't that the province of the controller?

Alas, it usually is. Which is just the point. For all a controller generally (and understandably, in light of the way ad spending has been rationalized in the past) knows about advertising, is that it frequently is the largest and by far the least tangible of the investments his firm makes. That advertising, even brilliant advertising, can all too easily be money down the drain. That he *mistrusts* it. With the unfortunate consequences that he avoids it (except to grumble), and keeps his breakevens to himself.

Yet if advertising spending *is* to be increasingly rational, somebody's got to pick up and use this concept in a systematic way in ad strategy development.

Defining breakeven as nothing more than total fixed costs (including advertising) divided by contribution margin (or the difference between sales price per unit and variable cost per unit), therefore, let's take the McCarthy Company again as an example (Exhibit 4.3).

From this we can see that the McCarthy Company is squarely on the horns of a dilemma. Not only is its bottom line volume sensitive and fixed food cost sensitive, but fixed costs are going through the roof, while volume is actually declining.

This latter point is puzzling, given McCarthy's new product formulation and size. Something important appears to be wrong with the McCarthy marketing program, in fact. And while we don't yet know what that is, it would be idle for the McCarthy advertising manager to propose either greater or lesser ad spending for the upcoming fiscal year without first finding out.

In fact, the McCarthy ad manager is playing dice for high stakes until the other executives of his firm, particularly its manufacturing and financial heads, come to his rescue. Those fixed cost increases have got to be understood and rectified before another (comparatively fixed) cost, advertising, is piled on top of them. Since rapidly rising fixed costs often signal basic plant inefficiency, the McCarthy Company may even have to undertake additional corrective fixed asset investments before advertising can really be given the green light to go after volume again.

I hope it is apparent from this just how important consideration of your company's breakeven characteristics can be to

Exhibit 4.3   Breakeven analysis of McCarthy's business indicates that its pyramiding fixed cost structure (at the Ft. Wayne plant particularly) is cutting sharply into profits

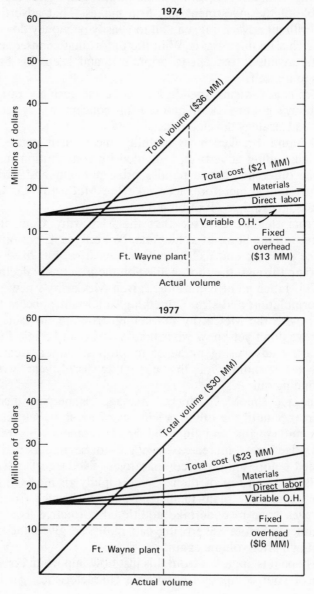

advertising strategy, compared to the "marketing only" approach many companies still limp along with.

Given the size of many advertising budgets, in fact, it frequently isn't enough to assess the overall breakeven characteristics of your firm or product, as we have done here. Rather, by developing breakevens on a market-by-market basis prior to establishing an advertising spending plan (a computer program will handle it easily), you can factor in the different pricing, media costs, sales costs, physical distribution costs, and changing product costs peculiar to each of your markets. And maybe find that an ad program that meets your profitability objectives in market A, fails in market B. Which might call for a whole series of marketing and advertising strategies, based on market-by-market realities.

Value Added Analysis

A third type of analysis that throws light on the economic realism of advertising is value added analysis. In this case, what you're primarily looking for from an advertising standpoint is an understanding of your company's current and potential role in the distribution of its products.

Before any reader gets put off by the mysterious term "value added," however, let me explain that the construction of such an analysis involves nothing more than an addition of the various costs and profit margins that accrue at each stage in the manufacturing and distribution of a product. Value added then denoting the difference between the landed cost of the product or its components at a given stage, and the price the product (to which value has been "added" through further processing or distribution steps) is shipped out at by the same stage.

A prerequisite for soundly financed advertising after all is an adequate margin structure. And if your stage in the manufacturing and distribution sequence of a product is not really "adding value" to the product, you are not likely to have such advertising or, by extension, control final user brand selection in your field either. Also, if trade margins in selling or distrib-

uting your product are not ample, or too ample, then the
trade's strategy in moving your product out through retail can
easily differ from your distribution strategy.

Thus, with our friends at the McCarthy Company we see
that while the company adds considerable value to the raw
materials it uses to make its furniture polish, both its profit
margins and its retailers' profit margins as a component of
the value they add are thin (Exhibit 4.4).

The McCarthy Company is, therefore, faced with another
problem. That is, in addition to its own thin margins, the margins the trade makes from its class of product are pretty nar-
row too.

Keep in mind that McCarthy sells its product through food
supermarkets—a type of retailer jealous about the shelf space
it allocates to different product categories, and with many
options to merchandise one product versus another. Also with
a history in recent years of hunting vigorously for higher
margin products, because of low supermarket chain profitability

· Thus, while the economics of the McCarthy Company
suggest that volume is especially important to it, the profit-
minded trade through which it retails has good reason for
being disenchanted with the profit McCarthy's product category provides. Therefore, trade support in terms of the favorable stocking, display, and newspaper featuring—always so
critical to the success of a product sold through supermarkets
—may be hard for McCarthy to come by.

About the most disheartening thing Mr. McCarthy could
hear right now, in fact, is that his major competitors enjoy
better margins than he does because of better manufacturing
economics. And that they are using these margins to offer extensive case allowances to the trade, by way of upgrading the
amount of in-store merchandising support their brands receive.
This might even call into Mr. McCarthy's mind the question
of trade willingness to keep three branded products on the
shelf in a product category as small as furniture polish. The
brand with the weakest consumer franchise and slowest recent

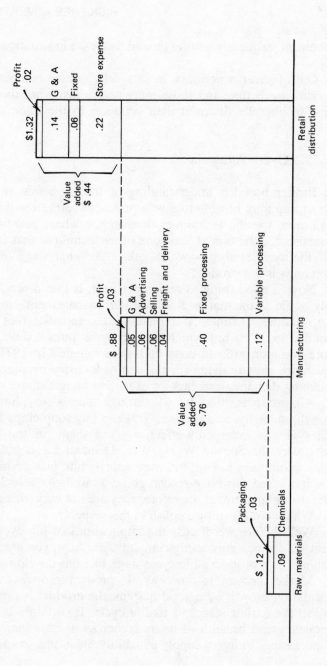

Exhibit 4.4 Value added per can of furniture polish

Retail distribution

$1.32
.14 — G & A
.06 — Fixed
.22 — Store expense

Profit .02

Value added $ .44

Manufacturing

Profit .03

$ .88
.05 — G & A
.06 — Advertising
.06 — Selling
.04 — Freight and delivery
.40 — Fixed processing
.12 — Variable processing

Value added $ .76

Raw materials

$ .12
.09 — Chemicals

Packaging .03

movement frequently getting the old heave-ho in situations like this.

Out of sheer orneriness, in fact, let's assume competitors' margins *are* better, and those margins are just what they are using to liberally discount their products to the trade.

Life Cycle Analysis

To further broaden understanding of the economic support advertising may be able to give a product (before considering even more specific techniques that suggest where and how to advertise it), there is at least one other technique that is useful: life cycle analysis—which asks, "At what stage of promotability is our product?"

Now, a good thing to remember here, is that a product is only as old as the market it serves, *plus* management's innovative qualities. Business is replete with companies that were founded in 1790 but which are peppy as pups today. Even more common are old dogs that were founded in 1970, but which are already dying for reasons of industry overcapacity, declining demand, and lack of executive imagination.

All products, that is, go through successive phases of growth, maturity, and decline. You *can* buy soap chips today. But synthetic detergents effectively ran them off the board right after the Second World War. Demand for double-knit fabrics continues to rise; but overcapacity and lack of innovation has killed this once golden goose as well. As vehicles for advertising investment, therefore, they are not very interesting.

What about furniture polish in this respect?

Well, before we discuss the implications of life cycle Exhibit 4.5 for our guinea-pig company, just how, you ask, is an estimate of a product's life cycle stage like this developed?

Market growth is one way. If product growth exceeds population growth by a good margin, the product is probably still in the earlier stages of its life cycle. It certainly is if the frequency and breadth of its usage across its customer group is increasing. Industry supply capability, including availability

Exhibit 4.5 Furniture polish market appears to be showing definite signs of maturity

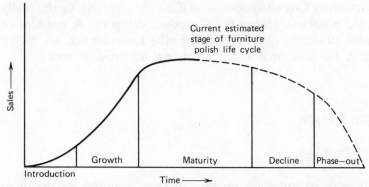

of supply for projected future demand levels, is another way.
And product development is a third. That is, can the product in
question be improved upon significantly? (In styling, in pricing, in performance features, in service?) *Is* it being improved
upon by innovative companies in its field?

The conclusions you reach about these signs of a product's
age are critical. Because in the process of coming to a decision
about them, you will be able to form a much better opinion
as to their reversibility. For some products, concentrated innovation can save the day. New and better uses can be found.
Better performance features and greater economy in manufacturing can be incorporated. Middle age can be extended.
Indefinitely sometimes. But for other products it may be too
late. If so, it's nice to know before you invest a lot of money
in advertising trying to change things.

By the way, do you happen to remember that we said both
the Bixbe Corporation and O'Shea Manufacturing, McCarthy's competitors, are giving away their margin structures to
the trade in return for merchandising support? Well typically,
that's not an effective long-term move for a mature product
trying to prolong its best days. Much more effective is the approach of promoting frequent usage of your product (as improved products tend to do) and finding new uses for it (as
smaller, trial-oriented sizes do).

In spite of some severe economic problems, therefore, and with a fairly advanced product life cycle to contend with, the McCarthy Company sounds as if it's the one making the really right economic moves in its product category. A rainbow of hope suddenly appears which, in the next chapter, we follow from the economic to the functional advertising area.

SUMMARY

Problem

By way of summarizing this chapter, it might be useful to pose a problem for the reader, calling on some of the points we have just discussed.

Specifically, what marketing strategy, including advertising strategy, might make sense for both company A and company B below, assuming that, as direct competitors, they displayed the following economic profiles? Assume, by the way, that company A is a public firm with the principal objective of increasing its earnings per share, and that company B is privately held, with sales growth the key objective.

RELATIVE ECONOMICS

	Company	
Economic factor	A	B
Current dollar sales	$324mm	$117mm
Breakeven point	$168mm	$ 64mm
Gross margin %	48%	45%
Contribution loss from a		
10% decline in margin	$ 16mm	$ 5mm

Solution. Company A loses far more dollars than B for every like percentage decline in margin each suffer. As a bigger company with a wider margin structure it probably has more absolute margin dollars to give up (although SG&A costs are unknown). Yet it needs those dollars to achieve its major corporate objective.

A's strategy should probably be to hold its pricing even at the risk of losing some volume, therefore. To do this, it may make sense to advertise heavily (advertising is cheap compared to what *A* stands to lose if it loses margin); develop new products (both for their consumer appeal and the wider margins they might offer); and strengthen its sales force, physical distribution, and customer service systems.

By contrast, a good strategy for *B* would be to exert price pressure in markets where *A* is most price sensitive or has its largest market shares. Discounts to wholesalers and retailers stocking *A*'s products (if such exist in this field), would also make sense in executing this strategy. To help fund this type program with its built-in margin decay, *B* might also try to develop higher margin products while ensuring that its advertising programs, service programs, and so on, are as fatfree as possible, to provide further margin cushion.

FIVE

SEQUENTIAL ANALYSIS: DEFINING THE SOURCES OF

Advertising Profit

The development of an investment-grade advertising strategy calls for more than just an analysis of the economic role advertising can play for a company, important and neglected as that phase of strategy development usually is. It calls for getting at that other major issue in advertising strategy, too. Namely, *from where and how will the profits made from advertising really come?*

While analysis of a firm's profit economics defines advertising's profit-making role, therefore, marketing-oriented analysis of a product line defines advertising's profit-making *sources*: by product and consumer type, by geographic region and channel of distribution, and by the specific marketing and advertising mix needed to elicit profits.

I said earlier, however, that the time-honored position review (at least as used by most companies of my acquaintance), leaves something to be desired as a tool for helping the planner perform this task. Therefore, I would now like to introduce an alternative technique for doing the same job: sequential analysis. This technique is illustrated in Exhibit 5.1.

Exhibit 5.1   Key questions and elements in the sequential
analysis of a product

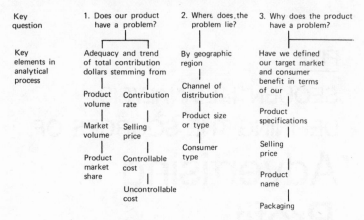

Exhibit 5–1 Key questions and alements in the sequential analysis of a product.

As I define it, sequential analysis is nothing more than an interrelated "probing for problems" that exist within the major profit-producing elements of a company's marketing system, with the objective of producing a logical flow of quantitative evidence to guide advertising strategy development.

Basically, this technique grows out of the conviction that it's unwise to brush the negative aspects of a product's marketing under a rug. And that in advertising, with its inherent risks, problems can provide at least as much useful information as successes and, when corrected, as much profit leverage as well.

Since the major profit-contribution elements in a company's marketing system vary of course from company to company, the precise elements used in the sequential analysis of different companies also vary. (For example, greater or lesser emphasis on sales force versus advertising analysis, depending on which, traditionally at least, has been more important in a firm's marketing mix.) For this reason, I have no urge to present sequential analysis, particularly in the single format we review, as a panacea.

Exhibit 5.1   (Continued)

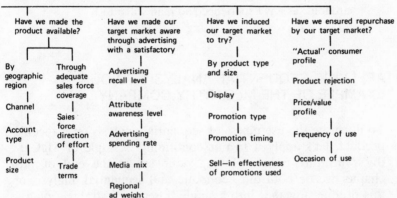

Have we made the product available?		Have we made our target market aware through advertising with a satisfactory	Have we induced our target market to try?	Have we ensured repurchase by our target market?
By geographic region	Through adequate sales force coverage	Advertising recall level	By product type and size	"Actual" consumer profile
Channel	Sales force direction of effort	Attribute awareness level	Display	Product rejection
Account type		Advertising spending rate	Promotion type	Price/value profile
Product size	Trade terms	Media mix	Promotion timing	Frequency of use
		Regional ad weight	Sell—in effectiveness of promotions used	Occasion of use

What I do argue versus the position review approach, however, is the following:

- Because the analytical framework used in sequential analysis is highly structured (literally sequential), it tends to approach advertising strategy development on its own terms. That is, as a process involving a selection between discrete action alternatives. (Under the position review approach you usually have to "find" the right answers to improved profitability. Here they tend to "drop out" for you.)
- Because sequential analysis emphasizes quantitative evidence, it can better relate advertising conclusions and action plans to actual volume and profitability developments. Furthermore, sequential analysis normally can be conducted with less than a half-dozen component quantitative techniques already well known to businessmen, namely:
  - Trend analysis
  - Segmentation analysis
  - Skew analysis

- Correlation analysis
- Comparative analysis
- Sequential analysis is less time consuming to use. This is important because the fact-gathering task that precedes advertising strategy determination is inherently tough and arduous, as any experienced ad man will attest.

APPLYING SEQUENTIAL ANALYSIS TO OUR EXAMPLE OF THE McCARTHY COMPANY

To illustrate the usefulness of sequential analysis on a specific product, let's apply it to our continuing example of McCarthy's furniture polish. Having done so, at the end of this chapter we tie both our economic and sequential analysis of this product together into a single, integrated strategic plan.

Also, as we discuss each one of the major issues that sequential analysis probes, the reader may wish to refer to the subissues (or key question elements) related to that issue, which are detailed in Exhibit 5.1. I suggest this to draw the reader's attention to the breadth of the analysis performed under a full-scale application of sequential analysis, which unfortunately must be abbreviated within the scope of this book.

Does Our Product Have a Problem?

Because the thrust of sequential analysis is to look for specific, hard, quantified evidence about a product's marketing problems, the measure it uses to gauge the existence and extent of those problems is profit contribution. That is, the difference between total product fixed costs and sales dollars. It does so because this measure is both discrete and flexible; it avoids entanglement with fixed cost allocations (although that question must eventually be solved within a company), while focusing on the contribution each product, type product, size product, and so on, in a line actually makes to profits.

The first question asked under sequential analysis, "Does our product have a problem?" is really designed, therefore, not only to define the existence of a problem, but also to characterize it in terms of the type constraints to profit contribution that exist. And, as I believe is apparent from Exhibit 5.1, such profit contribution problems can take two forms. First, those related to volume and share; and second, those related to selling price and costs, or profit contribution rate problems.

Experience suggests that attaining perspective on whether either of these is a problem for a brand, is primarily a question of looking at the trend of profit contribution on that brand. The analytical technique typically most useful within sequential analysis in determining the very existence and immediate financial source of a problem, therefore, is *trend analysis*, which simply looks at the direction and rate of change in a given variable, such as the business variable of profit contribution dollars shown in Exhibit 5.2.

Thus, as we might have suspected from our prior economic analysis (particularly our breakeven chart), McCarthy's profit contribution from its furniture polish is declining at a precipitous rate. The sharpness of its decline since the introduction of its new, improved product is a bit of a surprise, however. Moreover, current absolute profit contribution dollars look pretty paltry for a firm with a 30 million dollar sales level. Trend analysis in this instance has done a good job, in other words, not only of tackling the existence of a problem, but, in a financial sense, showing us it is a full-blown rather than emerging one.

Trend analysis typically does yeoman work in advertising strategy development, in fact, because by nature it not only describes the past, but suggests the future. It does not predict it, of course, because all future extrapolation of trends are ultimately based on judgment. Yet it certainly encourages the planner to probe further into those specific variables that point the way toward remedial action, as we can see in the further

Exhibit 5.2   The profit contribution the McCarthy company realizes from its furniture polish is declining fast

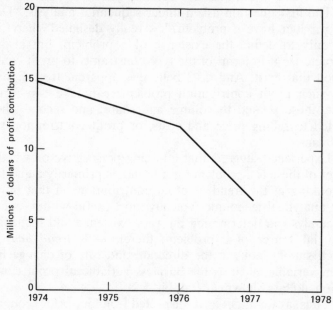

elaborations of the McCarthy Company's profit contribution problem shown in Exhibit 5.3.

Where Does Our Problem Lie?

We now have a line on those elements—volume, share of market, and contribution rate—that define the financial characteristics of the McCarthy Company's problem. As spelled out in the format at the beginning of this chapter, the second question in the sequential analysis of a product therefore focuses on the *location* of these problems. "Where does our problem lie?" By geographic region, by channel of distribution, by product type and size, and by type of customer.

Since each of these "location" factors generally represents a broad and complex variable, and since we must further cross-matrix each with McCarthy's three separate contribution problems to really locate the source of the problem in each instance, the quantitative tool most useful in the location issue is *segmentation analysis*, which simply breaks variables such as these down into their component parts for further examination.

Before I go further, however, I should probably mention to readers who do not have an advertising or marketing background, that segmentation in marketing primarily refers to different sets of customers, and that its range includes the following:

INDUSTRIAL MARKET SEGMENTATION

- Customer size
- Customer location
- Customer industrial classification
- Customer purchase characteristics (e.g., quantity, seasonality, features desired)

CONSUMER MARKET SEGMENTATION

- Demographic
- Geographic
- Psychographic
- Buyer behavior characteristics (e.g., usage rate, benefits sought, brand loyalty)

Hence the range of elements suggested for segmentation in our sequential analysis format, with the addition of segmentation by product type and size, simply because personal experience has proven that consideration of profit by product is too important to ignore.

And, after thoroughly segmenting the McCarthy business

Exhibit 5.3 The profit contribution problem on Mc-Carthy's furniture polish is one of declining volume (a), declining share (b) *and* a declining contribution rate (c)

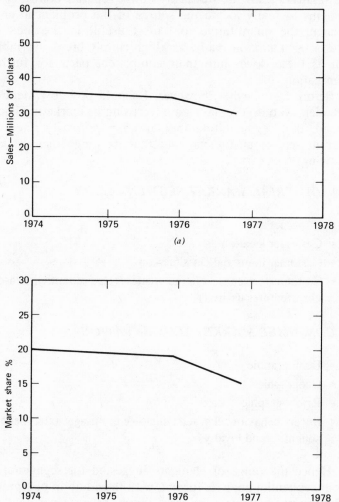

(a)

(b)

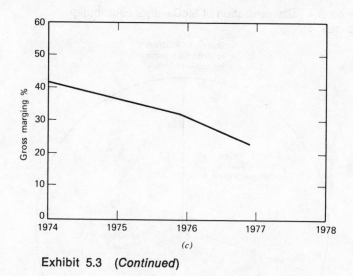

(c)

Exhibit 5.3 *(Continued)*

in a completely cross-matrixed way, we might find that McCarthy's contribution declines are concentrated in the smaller, Midwestern supermarkets it serves (Exhibit 5.4).

McCarthy's profit problems, therefore, are centralized within a specific geographic area and class of trade. This being the case, it would obviously be useful to know how much of the company's total business is located within that area and class of trade as well. Unfortunately, segmentation analysis can't tell us that; but *skew analysis* can.

Skew analysis (or "80/20" analysis, as it is sometimes called), is especially helpful in locating the source of a marketing problem, because by definition it looks at the concentrations in things: such as the concentrations in cost, volume, profit, and investment in a business. In so doing, it highlights the degree to which a company's advertising, for example, may have failed to help it move out to new markets or sales territories, or sell different customers, or make a dent in certain product categories, thereby relieving the undesirable market-

**Exhibit 5.4   Concentration of McCarthy's contribution
declines**

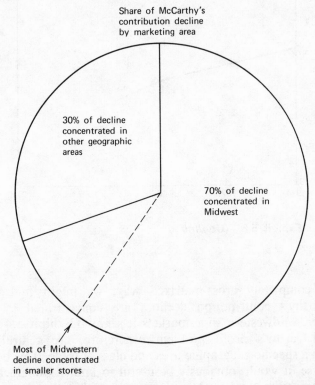

Share of McCarthy's
contribution decline
by marketing area

30% of decline
concentrated in
other geographic
areas

70% of decline
concentrated in
Midwest

Most of Midwestern
decline concentrated
in smaller stores

ing concentrations in a company's business. For example, see
Exhibit 5.5.

Now, if McCarthy's sales were actually moving ahead at
a decent clip, this lessened geographic concentration in its
business might be viewed as desirable by its management.
Perhaps greater geographic dispersal of sales is even a major
corporate objective. However, in McCarthy's case we know
that total sales between 1974 and 1977 were down. Therefore,
the whole ball game is somehow being lost in the Midwest, so
from now on, that's where we can principally focus our attention.

Exhibit 5.5   Only 42% of McCarthy's sales now come from its Midwestern sales region, compared to 65% three years ago

% U.S. Supermarkets and McCarthy Sales in Midwest

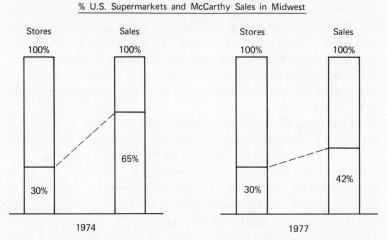

Incidentally, skew analysis often has "revelation" qualities like this. And what's more, of all the quantitative techniques normally used within sequential analysis, it is especially good at "price tagging" potential improvements advertising may be able to make. That is, because it deals in proportions (of volume, share, contribution, etc.), it directly sets up the possibility of calculating the profit improvement you get if you improve these proportions to levels you think more desirable and realistic for your product. For example, if advertising can help improve volume by 20%; or share by 15%, and so on.

Have We Defined Our Target Market And Consumer Benefit With Our Product?

Up to this point, we have concentrated on defining the nature and location of a product's problem. The real payoff from sequential analysis lies in its ability to discover *why* a product has a problem, however, thereby opening up a solution.

This action orientation starts right with the first question sequential analysis asks to probe the "why" issue: "Have we defined our target market and consumer benefit?" Not just theoretically, but through the product's actual specifications, its selling price, its name, and its packaging and service characteristics. Or, to put the question in perspective, are the basic physical, performance, and pricing attributes built right into the product telling the story management decided to tell, to the market it wanted it told to, when it first devised the product's charter?

This kind of question is important not only in terms of achieving corporate objectives, but also in terms of the special need in advertising today to project the innate character of a product to markets sincerely interested in that kind of character. Products in mature markets, especially, need to be differentiated from their competition in this way; as do products in what are fundamentally commodity-type markets— gasoline, soap, steel, banking, and so forth—where few real performance differences exist.

And, as with each of the major issues raised in sequential analysis, this one concerning the character of a product has a particularly useful technique associated with it for unlocking its answers. *Correlation analysis,* which tries in a systematic way to measure relationships between specific types of marketing activity (such as the features you've built into your product), and the volume and profit levels they produce. For example, see Exhibit 5.6.

Thus, as I think you may agree, sequential analysis is taking us down to bedrock on McCarthy's marketing problem pretty fast. We now know, for example, that not only does a serious problem exist, but also that it is affecting volume, share, and contribution rate to specific degrees; it is centered among a specific class of trade in the Midwest; and it has, as we've just found out, been caused (at least in part) by the company's puzzling failure to register those new and improved aspects of their product with consumers. All of which will make McCarthy's ultimate action response much more pointed and likely of sucess, which is just what the doctor ordered in a situation as threatening as this.

Exhibit 5.6 McCarthy sales areas showing largest percent declines in profit contribution correlate with failure
to register new product performance features instituted
last year

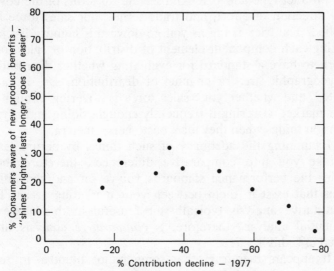

Have We Made Our Product Available?

Since the McCarthy Company's problem is at least partly
trade-related, the next question in sequential analysis is well
suited to that aspect of its problem. "Have we made our
product available?" Or, put colloquially, "Have we gotten
both the trade distribution and effort from our sales force
needed to pave the way for successful advertising?"

Productive advertising, after all, doesn't occur in a
vacuum. It must support, and be supported by, other elements
in your marketing mix. Especially by adequate product distribution (so there's something available for the ultimate
consumer to buy), and by what amounts to the other major
sales-getting tool in most companies, namely, its sales force.

Product availability merits inclusion as a key issue in sequential analysis, therefore, because it is a function of just

these two considerations. First, in terms of the adequacy of the retail or wholesale distribution a company has achieved by geographic area, by channel of distribution, and by account and product type and size. And second, in terms of the coverage, direction of effort, and trade terms your sales force has applied. The trick being as you go down this laundry list, analyzing each component element of distribution or sales force effort, to have a standard for evaluating whether distribution by geographic area or channel of distribution, say, is "adequate," and whether your sales force is covering enough of your market, covering it frequently enough, doing and saying the right things when they meet customers, etcetera.

Examining the adequacy of such things by nature tends to take you into comparative differences, therefore, both versus the performance standards you've set and the differences that exist in them between your marketing areas. The quantitative analysis typically most useful in this phase of sequential analysis, therefore, is *comparative* analysis illustrated in Exhibit 5.7.

It appears therefore, that some major blunder in redirecting the effort of the McCarthy Company sales force may also be responsible for the sales and profit declines occuring in the company's Midwestern stronghold. (In any event, advertising can never work efficiently against as low a base of distribution as is reflected in some of the trade areas below.) Perhaps Mr. McCarthy or his sales manager mistakenly felt the introduction of the new size and product was the right time to strike out for a broader geographic franchise, concentrating their sales and distribution efforts elsewhere, and taking the risk that pure product innovation would permit their polish to "sell itself" in their Midwest bailiwick.

In any event, those current out-of-stocks among small, rural supermarkets in the Midwest are horrendous. McCarthy will never retain product category leadership that way. And the McCarthy sales force probably must either be beefed up to provide true national coverage, or some of the boys called back from the "good-time areas" to get things going along the North Fork of the Chippewa once again.

Exhibit 5.7 Out-of-stocks of McCarthy's polish are higher in smaller, rural area stores in Midwest (*a*). This may be because sales force has been concentrating their call activity against larger retailers on East and West Coast plus Florida (*b*)

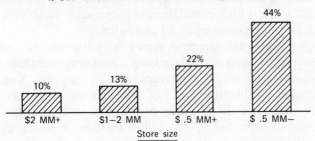

% Out—of—stocks in Midwestern sales region stores

Store size

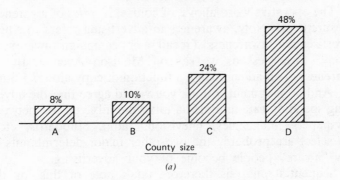

County size

(*a*)

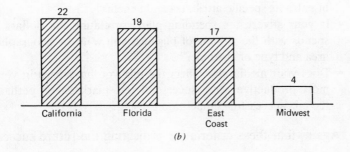

Average # sales calls per quarter on $1 MM supers since new product/size introduction

(*b*)

Have We Made Our Target Market Aware of Our Product and Its Benefits?

We said earlier that while advertising's sales and profit results are not adequately measurable, giant strides have been made in measuring the awareness advertising creates in the market. And that there is high correlation between such awareness and the sales-getting power of an ad campaign.

If you accept this premise, then I think it is also acceptable to argue that a *series* of advertising awareness measures may be an even better way to construct your ad program. You will still not get predictability out of this; but, through sort of a flanking action on the question of the sales and profit-producing power of advertising, you will at least get a better idea of what you should *try* to do in advertising.

The operative word above, of course, is *series* of awareness measurements. Now, awareness in advertising refers to single advertisement awareness (recall) or campaign awareness. "Copy" awareness as we say on Madison Avenue. But is awareness of an ad campaign a function of copy alone? I think not. And on judgment, I think you would agree that the advertising spending rate and media mix (the mix you use between newspapers, magazines, television, radio, billboards, etc.) you select are probably the two other major determinants of how "aware" people become of your advertising.

Sequential analysis therefore takes note of this, by the series of awareness-getting elements it sets up for investigation. That is:

- Is your copy creating awareness not only of your product but also its specific attributes and benefits?
- Is your advertising spending plan correlating the dollars it spends with the volume of business you want by geographic area and type of customer?
- Does your media mix reflect the mix you have used in your most productive area, successful test markets, or perhaps the mix successful competition is using?

Again, that these criteria for projecting the future success of an ad campaign are imperfect, I immediately concede. For one thing, awareness may correlate with sales, but it is *not* sales. For another, some of the same grab-bag of variables that affect the sales and profit measurement of advertising (competition by market, advertising costs by market, availability of good media by market) affect the level of awareness advertising achieves, too. Yet *far fewer important variables affect awareness than sales or profits* (product and physical distribution costs do not, trade distribution levels ipso facto do not, probably product pricing does not, either). Thus, while some variables can keep even extremely high awareness advertising from paying out, the awareness measures we suggest are both multiple in nature and "cleaner" in their evaluation than either sales or profit measurements.

Using some of the quantitive techniques we have already described, therefore, especially comparative and correlation analysis, the advertiser can through sequential analysis provide his management with a "weight of evidence" about what is apparently productive in the company's advertising, rather than just a Starch score (see Exhibits 5.8 to 5.11).

Have We Induced Our Target Market to Try Our Product? And Have We Ensured Repurchase by Our Target Market?

By now you may argee that sequential analysis is an acceptable name for this technique. Properly sequenced, and with a little bit of imagination supplied by the advertising planner, these analyses tend to support one another and unfold a total picture of a company. Who is it? What does it want? Where is it going? The whole "drama" of a company's character, motivation, and promotability, with supporting quantitative analyses providing as much of a fact-based story line as possible for the management reviewer. Perhaps even forcing him to reevaluate corporate objectives, if the hard evidence sequential analysis throws off ultimately supports such a case.

To ring down the curtain on sequential analysis, there are

Exhibit 5.8 Consumer recall of major benefit points in "new, improved" McCarthy ads has fallen below that of previous campaign levels

% Consumer Awareness

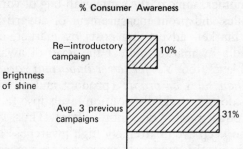

Brightness of shine

Re—introductory campaign — 10%

Avg. 3 previous campaigns — 31%

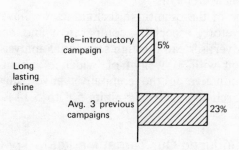

Long lasting shine

Re—introductory campaign — 5%

Avg. 3 previous campaigns — 23%

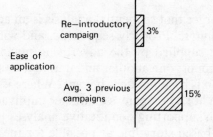

Ease of application

Re—introductory campaign — 3%

Avg. 3 previous campaigns — 15%

Exhibit 5.9   Longer-term awareness of McCarthy advertising has now fallen below that of Bixbe and O'Shea advertising

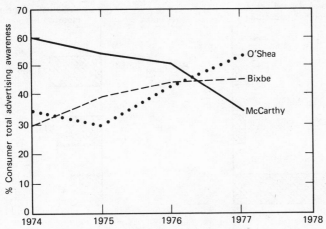

two final analytical sequences to consider. And, since they are so interrelated, we will consider them together. The first, "Have we induced our target market to try our product?" The second, "Have we ensured repurchase?"

The former question, "Have we gotten trial?" really asks if advertising is beng used in harness with a company's promotional tools: the type promotions it runs, the retail display it gets, the timing it follows on its promotions and, of course, which product it chooses to promote in the first place. The second question then focuses on the end-users who have tried the product while attempting to determine how they actually *are* using it (so advertising can correct this if it is not optimum); and why, in some cases, they are rejecting it (so either the product or its advertising can be geared to building more loyal users).

Initial trial on a product is, of course, important for two reasons. First, the kickoff of any consumer or industrial product in the market is usually critical to the long-term success of that product. As most experienced marketers would, I think,

Exhibit 5.10   McCarthy's advertising spending per thousand population for the last year has been lower in the Midwest than in other marketing areas, though media costs are comparable there

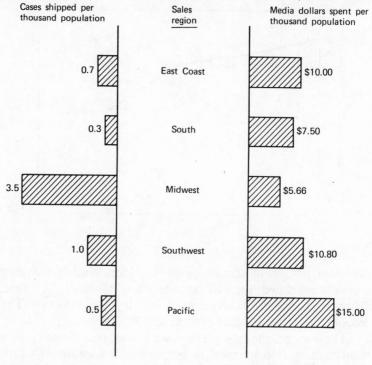

Cases shipped per thousand population	Sales region	Media dollars spent per thousand population
0.7	East Coast	$10.00
0.3	South	$7.50
3.5	Midwest	$5.66
1.0	Southwest	$10.80
0.5	Pacific	$15.00

agree, products that do not debut well do not age well; they have a nasty habit of not picking up steam later on. Distribution plays a part in this. The trade—any trade—usually comes down hard on a product that does not sell well from the outset, thereby helping its prophecy to become self-fulfilling.*

Initial trial is also important in that the promotional tools

* One of the few exceptions I can think of occurs in the motion picture business. There, "art pictures," designed with a limited audience in mind, are frequently introduced with little promotion in lower breakeven houses as a way of letting them "find their legs." Not many other products enjoy such a built-in system for permitting them to find their audience. They've got to come on galloping.

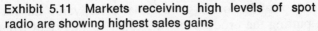

Exhibit 5.11 Markets receiving high levels of spot radio are showing highest sales gains

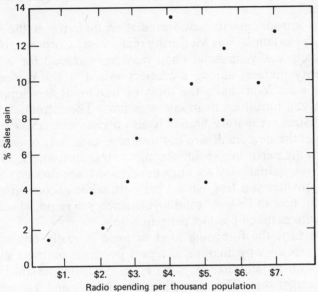

a company uses to get trial, and the way it uses them, can often cause or deny success to the whole marketing effort, at great expense. For instance, introductory couponing on a consumer packaged goods product can easily cost millions. However, if such a promotion is out of sync with adequate distribution levels achieved before the coupons are distributed; if introductory advertising on the product hasn't built to satisfactory awareness levels; or if the trade isn't properly prepared by the sales force to display and otherwise merchandise the product during the key redemption period, then the whole advertising and promotional blast can itself be either blown or muffled. The mechanisms, timing, and coordination of the promotions you use to get trial walk a fine and expensive line.

The specific products promoted and the type promotion applied are also important in getting the right market to try—as they are in setting up repurchase. If handled well, that is, they can provide both a good initial price/value impression, while putting the product in "interested" hands right from the outset.

In introducing its new formulation *and* size at the same time, for example, was McCarthy really wise? Corporate objectives, especially financial ones, may have argued for it. The majority opinion among marketers would, I think, run the other way. You make the most of important developments when you introduce them one at a time. The introduction of small sizes on mature brands is also a risky enterprise unless you get the new small size out to a new audience, or satisfy a clearly lighter-using group among current customers. Otherwise, you actually induce current users to trade down to a size that provides you less income per unit, while encouraging the faithful user to be less brand loyal (since you're not "loading" him with as much product per purchase).

In fact, the foregoing kind of logic is really one of the chief reasons why analysis of repeat purchase patterns should start with a definition of your "actual" customer rather than your target one. They can differ startlingly; and knowing if you're off base on this critical user question is the only way to really find out whether you've made a mistake that will force you to change your marketing program; or, as sometimes happens, find that you're actually benefiting by a better class of usage than you actually bargained for, thereby encouraging you to *really* get aggressive with the product. Either way, you find yourself right back at corporate objectives at this point. Do you want 'em or don't you?

By contrast, advertising can be made to address itself to product usage and rejection questions fairly easily. In part because the data on which advertising responses to such questions can be shaped—readily buyable usage and attitude studies—are usually both statistically reliable and highly directive.* But *whom* you choose to do business with is

---

* For example, "Usage of our lipstick is off 20% among women 18–25, primarily because our 'junior market' shades are wrong this season. Therefore, next year we will both widen our shade line and allocate greater attention to this feature in our television commercials."

another matter. A judgmental matter, even after the analysis is in. And the very factor that makes sequential analysis a reiterative process too, because you can never give up analyzing your business if you're not happy with your buyer.

Our friends at McCarthy? Perhaps they won't be happy either after finding that the trial level of McCarthy's new small size has been low, and, in part, this weak trial level correlates with consumer confusion about the type of person who should use this size, as illustrated by Exhibits 5.12 and 5.13.

Exhibit 5.12   The trial level of McCarthy's new small size has been low

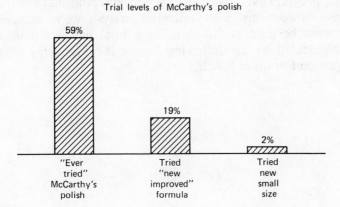

Trial levels of McCarthy's polish

Exhibit 5.13   In part, this weak trial level correlates with consumer confusion as to type of person who should use this size

% Consumers trying small size by perceived purpose of size

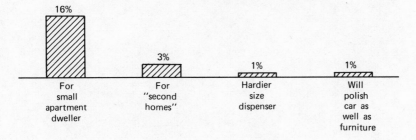

SUMMARY

The analytical techniques we have just described for developing fact-based ad programs obviously involve a dedicated commitment to getting a satisfactory return from advertising by all the members of a management team.

If this method, or some reasonable simplification of it (for example, a collection and analysis of the relevant facts without so much formal exhibitry), still seems too long or hard, alternatively all I can seriously suggest is that the advertiser can go back to some greater or lesser degree of guessing about whether his ad program really pays.

Keep in mind, too, that the habit of using facts to develop an ad program gets easier as time goes on. And that the techniques of economic and sequential analysis we've described can even be used as the basis for a total business plan, as, demonstrated by the following layout for McCarthy's New Improved Furniture Polish.

Exhibit 5.14 An example of sequential analysis.

Sequential analysis on these key issues	Leads to these analyses	These conclusions	These opportunities	And these strategies
Does our product have a problem?	Trend analysis of the product's profit contribution over time.	Controller's Dept. analysis indicates product's profit contribution is steadily declining.	Profit contribution and volume declines can be halted, and probably reversed. Fixed manufacturing problem can also be rectified by new equipment investment. (Manufacturing and Finance agree with both of these conclusions.)	Launch major advertising and sales effort aimed at regaining lost volume, share, and pricing realization, in keeping with company's historical objective of being the largest and most "savvy" company in its field. Back this effort up with investment spending to regain satisfactory manufacturing capacity and economics. (Projected breakevens show these are attractive enough risks to meet corporate risk criteria.)
	Trend analysis of product volume, market volume, and market share.	Market Research reports market growth remains healthy, but our product's volume and share are declining.		
	Trend analysis of product contribution rate, selling price, controllable and uncontrollable costs.	Again, Controller reports contribution rate per unit sold is declining *fast*. Problem is that recent price increase not being observed and unit costs at Ft. Wayne plant (according to the V.P. Manufacturing) are skyrocketing because of lowered volume and higher fixed costs.		

67

Exhibit 5.14 *(Continued)*

Sequential analysis on these key issues	Leads to these analyses	These conclusions	These opportunities	And these strategies
Where does the problem lie?	Segmentation analysis based on above findings to define where problem lies by geographic area, channel of distribution, specific product/ consumer type, or manufacturing process/facility.	Joint Marketing/Finance analysis indicate volume and contribution rate problems are concentrated among retailers located in Midwest. Manufacturing also reports our Ft. Wayne manufacturing plant is only center of fixed manufacturing cost increases.	Volume from Midwest sales area can be increased. New investment to improve operating economics of Ft. Wayne plant will payout within acceptable time span if lost volume is recaptured.	Direct increased proportion of next year's advertising and sales efforts at Midwestern districts. (I.e., traditionally the firm's "high franchise" territory.)
	Comparative analysis to measure how we are doing on each of above factors versus competition.	O'Shea Manufacturing showing greatest competitive volume increases following opening 2 years ago of their new Gary, Indiana, plant.		
	Skew analysis to determine the degree of product's sales concentration by region, channel, and product/ consumer type.	42% of sales come from Midwest region compared to 65% 3 years ago. Major decline also apparent among smaller retailers in Midwest,		

Have we defined our target market and consumer benefits?

Comparative and correlation analysis to determine if target market is being reached with desired product benefit through the product's
Physical and performance characteristics
Selling price
Name
Packaging and service programs.

Computer center reports share, sales, and profit declines are correlated only with failure to register new product performance features instituted last year. In areas where these features have gained recognition, no trouble has been experienced in realizing recent price increase.

More sharply focused advertising and sale efforts hold the possibility not only of reversing volume down-trend, but also of increasing profit contribution significantly through maintenance of price advance.

Stay with new product formulation, name, packaging, and pricing while focusing on improvements in advertising and sales activities.

Refocus sales efforts to provide greater trade awareness of these features in problem market territories.

Exhibit 5.14 (*Continued*)

Sequential analysis on these key issues	Leads to these analyses	These conclusions	These opportunities	And these strategies
Have we made our product available to our target market?	Analysis of comparative distribution by geographic area, channel, account type, and product type/size.	Sales Department indicates that retail out-of-stocks are high throughout Midwest, but especially in smaller stores located in rural areas.	Redirection of sales force effort to obtain more uniform distribution, product stocking, and awareness of new dealer margin structure, will provide the first step toward regained profitability.	Revise sales coverage, small account call frequency, and possibly presentation methods to build trade awareness of new product features and margin advantages. Get distribution problem fixed before more money is spent on consumer advertising.
	Comparative analysis of sales force coverage by region, sales force direction of effort, and trade terms versus those of competition.	Sales force has been concentrating their call frequency on disproportionate basis against larger retailers on East and West Coast plus Florida. Sales Manager believes new trade terms are attractive to all retailers but still not widely known in Midwest problem area.		

Have we made our target market aware of our product and its benefits?	Total awareness of our product and its specific attributes among our target customers.	Awareness of our advertising has fallen below that of both O'Shea Mfg.'s and the Bixbe Corporation's national ad programs. Awareness declines again concentrated in the Midwest.	Heavy-up of media spending against low performance areas offers promise of rebuilding volume in those areas. Revised advertising copy and media mix also appear to offer significant leverage for improving both price increase observance and consumer volume.	Have ad agency prepare revised media plan including national plan that heavies up radio spending proportionate to total budget, and rural Midwest markets proportionate to balance of U.S. Also request that agency undertake preparation of new advertising copy that registers in a more memorable way the benefit characteristics of new product.
	Consumer recall of our advertising and specific elements within it.	Consumer recall of new campaign is well below recall levels of past advertising executions.		
	Correlation of our advertising spending rate with our sales level by marketing area.	Ad spending throughout Midwest significantly below that of other areas as expressed as index of per thousand population by area.		
	Comparative analysis of the sales getting power of our advertising by media used to disseminate our message.	Markets receiving high levels of spot radio spending and message weight plus trade direct mail effort are showing highest sales gains.		

Exhibit 5.14 *(Continued)*

Sequential analysis on these key issues	Leads to these analyses	These conclusions	These opportunities	And these strategies
	Comparative analysis of our advertising spending by sales region versus that of competition, and correlation of these results with our sales levels.	Ratio of our spending to competitive levels shows we are being heavily outspent in rural areas. However, correlation between our media spending to deceased volume on our product is greatest where our own spending falls under $10 per thousand population, not where we are heavily outspent by competition.		

| Have we induced our target market to try our product? | Comparative analysis of the trial levels of our product within our target market, broken down by
Product type or size
Promotion mechanisms used, including product display at retail level
Promotion timing used
Promotion sell-in effectiveness to the trade. | Trial level of new product formulation is weak on new small size. This weakness further correlates with sales areas that have not received "2 for price of 1" introductory promotion. | Application of trial promotion effort aimed at getting distribution of new size has shown excellent payout characteristics. | "Re-introduce" the new product in low performance areas that have not received the successful sell-in promotion. Include initial promotion and/or others similar to it in this corrective effort. |

73

Exhibit 5.14 *(Continued)*

Sequential analysis on these key issues	Leads to these analyses	These conclusions	These opportunities	And these strategies
Have we insured repurchase by our target market?	Analysis of extent of product or price value rejection of our product. Analysis of frequency and occasion of use of our product. Analysis to determine whether "actual" customer profile correlates with target consumer characteristics.	MR's special U & A study indicates that consumers are having no difficulty appreciating price/value trade-offs of our improved product. However, range of potential uses of our new small size not yet completely understood.	New advertising that pinpoints small size usage potential may help bolster consumer demand and subsequent trade stocking patterns.	Have agency include attention to new small size uses in their revised copy strategy and advertising executions.

74

| How do our profit economics affect our ability to compete with this product? | Sensitivity of product profits to changes in volume, pricing, mix, cost, and investment. | Controller's sensitivity analysis indicates greatest need is to maintain volume. Sufficient sensitivity to new pricing structure and fixed costs exist for us to "go after" improvements in those areas as well. | Total dollar profit and ROI can be increased to planned levels if new promotion program is successful. | Investment spend to rectify advertising, sales, and manufacturing shortcomings, and put company back in position to enjoy available promotional investment leverage. |
| | Effect of efficiency of facilities (breakeven) on our ability to compete with this product. | Unless principal manufacturing line at Ft. Wayne plant is speeded up through new machinery, plant will be uneconomic within 2-year period says V.P. Manufacturing. V.P. Finance acknowledges that investment potential of these improvements is clearly sufficient for us to increase our debt/equity ratio. | Manufacturing constraint at Ft. Wayne can be alleviated at acceptable cost level. | Initiate Ft. Wayne manufacturing line improvements. |

Exhibit 5.14. (Continued)

Sequential analysis on these key issues Leads to these analyses	These conclusions	These opportunities	And these strategies
Effect of our position in the industry (value added) on our ability to compete in this market.	Well-entrenched retailers in our field increasingly calling for wider margins, and dropping lines that do not respond. We could lose 20–30% more distribution unless this problem is rectified within next 12–24 months.	Planned sales, advertising, and manufacturing improvements should permit us to widen margins sufficiently to meet current retailer demands. However, longer-term we must seek to create greater consumer "pull" rather than dealer "push."	Continue to monitor and "price tag" benefits that revised promotional and business strategy actually provides. Correct strategic directions as dealer demands change and cash flow situation improves.

SIX

Organizing for

ADVERTISING

It isn't always easy to know if you're getting the kind of management coordination you need to substantially reduce advertising risk. For one thing, advertising problems don't pop out at you from organization charts.

Rather, it's the leadership and management processes *behind* the charts that distinguish successful from unsuccessful companies in developing sound advertising strategy. In fact, the type organizational structure you choose is rarely *the* major factor in determining whether your company achieves a strategic orientation to its advertising.

As we discussed briefly in an earlier chapter, the reason for this is simple. Successful advertising, like successful marketing, is more a focus than a function. And a clear focus on what your market really wants, and how you can honestly supply it, is far more likely to result from how objective, innovative, and hard working your executives are, not how they're boxed.

Still, you must choose some form of organization for your advertising. And normally, this results from the type of marketing organization you choose. Which can follow functional, product, or market lines as shown in Exhibit 6.1.

Exhibit 6.1   The three major types of marketing—and
advertising—organization: functional (*a*), product (*b*)
and market (*c*)

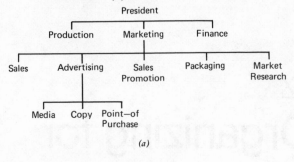

(*a*)

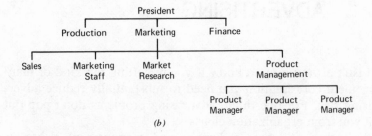

(*b*)

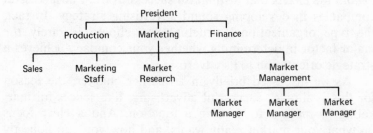

(*c*)

Up to the early 1960s, there was no doubt. The functional
organization prevailed in the vast majority of companies. Since
that time, the Byzantine-like proliferation of product lines
that has occurred in the American economy has changed all
that. Americans now, for example, have 124 makes and mod-

els of automobiles, 332 types of semiconductors and even 56 brands of bathroom tissue to choose from.

If there *is* a point to be made about advertising organization in this book, however, it's this. Not only is the functional system of organization the oldest and simplest way of organizing for advertising, but there are good reasons for thinking that, if one system *does* have an advantage, it's the functional, even in situations involving long and complicated product lines.

THE ADVANTAGES OF A FUNCTIONAL SYSTEM

The most important advantage of the functional system of organization may be this. Within this type of organization, responsibility for business planning and capital deployment is placed at the top, with the president and other experienced managers of your firm. For, presumably, these are the best people, not only to contribute to the type of multifunctional strategic thinking that advertising requires, but also to direct the execution of your ad program once it has been developed.

A functional system also offers the important secondary benefit of backing up top management with experienced specialists in copy, media, research, and promotion, *without* the line/staff arguments that frequently occur under a product or market manager system.

By contrast, within the product or market-based form of organization, strategy is both developed and executed under the leadership of a "mini-president." A product or market manager, who, granted his youthful enthusiasm and proprietary interest in his sphere of operations, usually lacks the the experience *and* authority to make binding decisions over functional areas in his business, or even the sales force selling his product.

Under either of these latter forms of organization, in other words, both strategy development and execution are the province of someone who is essentially a planner, not a line manager. And someone you cannot really measure on a P&L basis, because: (a) he does not typically have line authority over any expense except advertising; and, (b) he generally shares what authority he has with staff specialists. (Who frequently are more interested in graduating to the product or market manager's job than perfecting their own, current specialties.)

Obviously, I am not saying a product or market system cannot produce good advertising. It can, especially when staffed by talented and strategic-minded people. What I *am* saying is this. Advertisers who elect for either of these forms of organization might well ask themselves if the major negative inherent in them is not the same that they themselves frequently object to in their advertising agencies. Namely, management by managers who, through no fault of their own, have not yet completed their internship.

The question arises, however, doesn't the growing complexity of a business frequently *necessitate* a move to a product or market manager system? The answer, I think, is no. For experience suggests a functional system can be very effective in handling most (not all) types of promotional complexity.

For example, if advertising clearly dominates the marketing mix in your company, or a single product line accounts for most of your sales and profits, do you really want to delegate responsibility for this key function or product category down-the-line? If you do, you may be putting the fate of your whole company in the hands of a young generalist.

A functional organization is also well suited to your needs when you market a series of major product lines. Two good examples are General Motors and ITT, which have created several giant, functionally organized divisions to retain the advantages of senior management involvement over large and important pieces of their business.

Last, a functional organization is appropriate to a company's needs when it sells a line of similar products to the same basic market. (A cosmetics company is a classic example. Such a company tends to sell an overall line—lipstick, mascara, nail polish, etc.—to the same consumer, through the same trade channels in each case.)

Therefore, it is not the number of products you sell but whether those products require one overall promotional strategy or many that probably determines which type advertising organization is best for you.

WHEN A COMPANY MUST USE A PRODUCT/MARKET SYSTEM

Suppose, however, your product line does require the development of separate advertising strategies. That you are a toilet articles producer, for example, and you market distinct product lines (toothpaste, headache remedy, hair tonic, deodorant) to different end-use markets through a variety of trade channels.

Well, then it is especially important to realize that management coordination will be a *critical* determinant of the success or failure of your advertising. And you must be sure that you have an organized strategy development process that molds the ideas and insights of your various functional managers into a coherent promotional plan too.

You must also be careful to avoid the substitution of executional for strategic review in your advertising control process under either of these more complex forms of organization. Otherwise, your product's strategic course will keep changing direction from one progress review to the next, as your young "mini-president" knocks himself out spending as much time satisfying top management's nit-picking comments as their important, strategic ones.

In fact, if at your next advertising progress review meeting under any of these organizations, you find your top management group more concerned with whether individual ads are good or bad, whether headlines are too large or too small, and is it right to be in *Better Homes and Gardens* in the first place, you can be pretty sure that your organizational system isn't working for you. And what's worse, you've lost the emphasis on strategy execution (or revision) in which such meetings should deal.

Which is deadly under any kind of system.

SEVEN

WHY YOU MAY BE
Spending Wrong

When you realize that your advertising costs may equal or exceed your net profit after tax, the importance of how you set your ad budget quickly sinks in.

Advertising budget setting is complicated too. Not only must you decide the overall size of your budget, but also how you will allocate it geographically, across your product line, and in harness with your other marketing tools—all in support of your overall advertising strategy. Moreover, when it comes to advertising, nature dislikes a tightwad almost as much as a spendthrift. For while overspending can lead to Chapter XI, underspending leads to opportunity loss.

For example, one of the consistent mistakes advertisers make is to spend high on the hog when times are good, then cut back severely when business conditions deteriorate. Yet beyond a certain message level advertising becomes irritating; while the Morrill research we have already reviewed strongly suggests that if you don't spend consistently you won't do as well as your more persevering brethren.

Several conclusions therefore emerge. Ad budget thinking is serious management thinking; your advertising budget (just like your advertising strategy) must be part of your company's overall business plan; and spending techniques that help make advertising an efficient profit-making tool, really *must* be used.

The problem is, the traditional methods of setting an advertising budget are either illogical or incomplete, leading to both inefficiency and a vague lack of confidence on the part of many advertisers in the use of advertising. In this chapter, therefore, I review the major budget-setting techniques, pointing out their strengths and weaknesses. Then I suggest an alternative composed of the best features of each, plus some practical advice based on experience.

THE TRADITIONAL ALTERNATIVES

You deal in several issues when you set an advertising budget. These are: affordability, competitiveness, objectives, risk, and efficiency. Not surprisingly, each of the traditional ways of setting a budget responds to one or more of these issues, although none do on a completely satisfactory basis.

The Percentage of Sales Method

The most common way of setting an ad budget is the percentage of sales method. This is the one that says that last year our sales were X, and this year they are expected to be Y. Therefore, we can afford to take a percentage of Y and call that our ad budget.

In spite of the enormous popularity of this simple and comprehensible way of setting a budget, the fact remains: there is next to no logic—or strategy—in it. For one thing, if market demand falls off considerably, and you scale your advertising budget down to your new sales expectations, how do you know your reduced dollars will buy enough *message weight* to make your voice heard in the market? People react to the number of messages you send them after all, not to what a dollar spending formula says you can afford. Con-

versely, if your nonadvertising costs rise more steeply than
demand, an inflexible commitment to your initial percentage
of sales commitment could put you in the red.

In fact, it's easy to point out the dilemmas this method
creates, mainly because it assumes that advertising is *not* a
causal factor of sales and profits. Or, at best, that advertising
produces its effects in a linear fashion, on the basis of dollars
spent. Which is a pretty discouraging premise to start with,
particularly if you view advertising as a high leverage and
basically strategic operation.

The Competitive Level Method

This method assumes that if you spend about the same as
competition, or in proportion to your market share, you will
avoid being "blotted out" by enemy action. Unfortunately, it
also is a technique that has too many faults to be used as anything other than a check on the general adequacy of your
budget.

For one thing, like the percentage of sales method, it dis-
regards the *quality* of everyone's advertising, including your
own. Yet the real secret of being an effective advertiser is to
make all that hard strategic thinking you've done result in
supremely creative ads, which can make $100,000 go as far as
a million. Second, who's to say that past levels of competitive
expenditure indicate what future ones will be? And third, who
says competition was right in the first place? For example,
their spending may be nowhere near a "threshold of effectiveness" on a message weight basis. Or maybe it's excessive in
this respect.

The competitive method also leads to inflexibility in budgeting the rest of your marketing mix, because the defensive
objective of "matching" competition in advertising takes precedence over having balanced marketing program. Thus, your
total promotional program can easily be crippled. But if it is,
chances are your advertising will be crippled too. About the
best to be said for this method, in fact, is that analysis of com-

petitive spending patterns may tell you what *their* advertising strategy is, thereby providing a free "test market" from which you can shape certain limited aspects of yours.

The Task Method

Under the task method, management sets objectives (e.g., market share, sales, brand awareness) for advertising to accomplish, then *judgmentally* determines a budget for achieving these objectives.

This method has some good points.

For one thing, it forces you to think about your advertising objectives. It therefore tends to integrate advertising into your overall strategic plan. It also promotes a *long-term* investment approach to marketing, when that approach is relevant. (For example, when the way to maximize your return from advertising is to build to a dominant market share first, then "milk" profits later on.)

The major failing with the task method, however, is that it too overlooks the need for an in-depth strategic analysis of a company as an organic precondition to setting a budget, and therefore begs the issue. *Are the objectives worth the cost?*

The Breakeven Method

By this time you may agree that the major shortcoming of most advertising budget systems is that they are either too formularized or too judgmental. They pay little attention to what is unique about a company or product, particularly in terms of its controlling profit economics and potential profit sources.

Thus, while the breakeven method also has its flaws, its ability to quantify how much you can potentially make (or lose) by different levels of advertising (and even assumed levels of sales response from that advertising) puts it head and shoulders above the other systems. Particularly in dealing with the issue of the risk associated with a given spending level.

What *is* the breakeven method? In a nutshell, it's one that attempts to quantify the advertising spending level at which your company will make the greatest net additional gross profit. This objective can be best described graphically as in Exhibit 7.1.

Obviously, what the breakeven method does (call it the net additional gross profit method if you wish) is to force you (either in your sequential analysis or later) to search the facts of past or test markets to determine the gross margin dollars produced by different combinations of advertising variables, including different spending levels.

Having done this (or having launched new test spending markets to find out), you can make the prima facie assump-

Exhibit 7.1 Empirically derived estimates of gross profit in XYZ company at different advertising spending levels

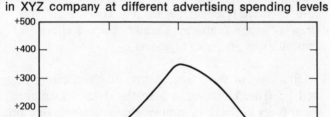

tion that your future sales and profit response curves will follow the same pattern, *if* the marketing variables that apply are reasonably similar to what they were in the historical or test period.

The major objections to the breakeven system, of course, are that

- Not enough past or test data may be available, thereby forcing you to spend a good deal of time perfecting this spending system before you can profit from it.
- A company may not have the necessary investment funds to force the marginal contribution curve to its maximum, even if it can predict the curve. That is, a company may simply not have the financial reserves to spend at the level that experience or testing says will give it the optimum return from its advertising.
- The multiplicity of variables in an advertising situation, including ones over which you have no control (like competitive spending), could negate any conclusions you might draw as to the future applicability of past efforts (i.e., the "test markets are junk" argument).

The first two of these arguments, in given circumstances, may well be true. However, where the data is available, and time permits its collection, simply going through this process helps develop an excellent fact-based assessment of what's right and what's wrong with your advertising program.

For example, one aspect of your analytical program might be to review the impact of various past spending *and* message weight variations on each of your geographic, product, and end-use markets. This can pinpoint where your sales response across these factors has been best; where your advertising agency has been buying media efficiently, thereby improving the breakeven characteristics of individual markets; and where your spending has been above or below a level warranted by market potential.

The breakeven method, as mentioned earlier, also is a superb tool for highlighting where you can't reach an adequate profit in a market because excessive media, distribution, or other costs in that market make a satisfactory gross margin performance virtually impossible for you. For examples of this see Exhibits 7.2 and 7.3.

The differences in market profitability shown by Exhibit 7.3, for example, mean you either get more persuasive advertising copy or change your marketing mix in certain markets. (This type analysis is, of course, especially important in new product introductions, where product costs change quickly with volume, product formulation changes, etc.) While the breakeven method is not a panacea, therefore, it is easily the most *diagnostic* of the budget setting processes. Which is just what the doctor ordered to get rid of some of that "rule of thumb" decision-making that continues to characterize most ad budgeting systems.

Exhibit 7.2 Markets spending $20.00–25.00 per thousand population in advertising correlate with XYZ company's highest advertising profitability levels

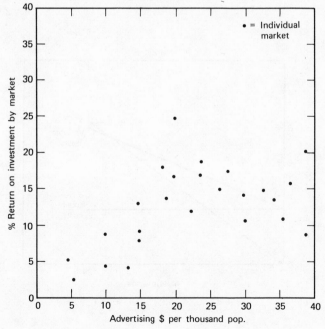

Exhibit 7.3 Profitability of even $20.00 per thou-
sand population spending areas can differ because
of individual market breakeven characteristics

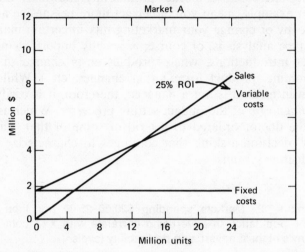

Market A

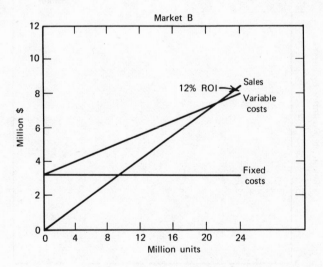

Market B

THE IMPORTANCE OF ALLOCATION

Once you've figured out *what* to spend in advertising, you're ready for the other half of the battle. *Where* to spend.* The where to spend question being, very arguably, the more complicated of the two. It is also the one for which you, as the most knowledgeable party about the geographic distribution of your business potential, must bear a leadership role.

The fact of the matter is that many advertising agencies are especially poor on the conceptual job of defining a system for the geographic or end-use deployment of advertising monies anyway. The problem being that most agency media departments are so overwhelmed with the paperwork of buying media these days, that they have cut back on their media thinkers and have staffed with paper processors. So unless your account executive has a good head for media allocation, you must plan on carrying the major share of the load yourself.

Before you get hot and bothered at the unfairness of this, remember that the allocation problem is not insurmountable, just tricky. Primarily because there are so many ways *to* allocate. For example, you can spend according to already developed end-use business patterns; according to your estimate of undeveloped potential by market area; or, to support business patterns as they are currently unfolding.

There are also an almost infinite number of variations to these. You can "lead" the business slightly in your most productive markets and spend roughly proportionate to it in the remaining ones; you can spend heavily in selected markets that hold special potential, and risk business decay elsewhere; you can spend where you are not really sure of potential but where your demographics are right. And so on.

* I am consciously leaving out of this book the *how* to spend question, i.e., what media. Addressing this issue, I believe, is primarily an agency management task, with the answer proceeding from the character of your message, the relative efficiency of different media in reaching your target customers, and the trade merchandising value of each media. All of which are areas presumably more in your agency's area of competence than your own.

To find your way out of this maze, however, there is really only one guide. And that is to approach media allocation as a logical process. For example, the first thing you must consider is one of the key facts you will have pinned down in your sequential analysis, anyway. Namely, *where your sales and marginal contribution dollars are really coming from.*

As discretely as possible, therefore, and preferably by individual media market, it's wise to make this data your chief criterion for allocation, particularly if current success is what you choose to follow. (Which could be a very good thing to follow if your established markets are providing you with the ROI, dollar profit, or favorable competitive situation you want, and if you are producing up to plant capacity as well.)

Second, *try to define your remaining potential in established markets.* It's also wise, after all, to look at every dollar spent in advertising as an incremental dollar, freshly put at risk as you spend it. Other things (distribution, sales force coverage, media costs, etc.) being equal, it may therefore make sense to risk some business decay in current markets to spend dollars against larger hunks of potential that your business analysis has suggested are developable. In other words, spending situations that offer you a better tradeoff of dollars spent for potential dollars earned.

Third, look at what is adequate in a message weight sense. What's message weight? Simply the application of the so-called "reach and frequency" concept, which any good agency —including yours—should already be applying to your media schedule anyway. (At least if you advertise in consumer media.)

In brief, all this involves is the estimating, through formal media research, of the percentage of your target audience that you are reaching with your advertising messages, and the number of times over a given period (e.g., a month) you are reaching them.* For again, bear in mind that consumers do

---

* Compared to this method, the "gross impressions count," or total number of readers or viewers exposed to your advertising, is for the birds. Unless you're simply trying to impress the trade, of course.

not respond to advertising dollars spent, hard-won though they may be. They respond to the sales messages they actually see or read, and the frequency with which they are exposed to them, which is a function of media costs by market and how cheaply your agency can buy.

In this connection, I once, for example, got a client to accept what he considered to be a major risk of business deterioration, by moving a large amount of his total advertising dollars from one set of markets to another less well established group. Behind my recommendation, however, was an analysis that pretty much proved we could run a lower, *sustaining* level of message weight in established markets, while enjoying the tactical flexibility of more messages in what till then had been markets we couldn't afford. The fact that it worked proves that, while fishing in market areas where the fishing is good probably has the best track record of success in spending advertising monies, carefully considered programs to fix problem markets can produce solid results too.

4 FINAL RULES

Having recognized the complexity of the overall media budget-setting and allocation task, including the amount of time it may take for you to get the breakeven method "up to speed" because of its data requirements, what approach generally does make sense? Again, let's deal in processes rather in formulas.

1. *Use a combination of the task and breakeven methods to the extent that readable past advertising experience keeps you from going all the way with the breakeven system.* At minimum you should be able, from your normal control system, to reliably construct the cost side of the market-by-market breakevens you require. If in some markets your volume requirements to reach the profit levels you want then seem too horrendous, no matter what assumption you make about your

advertising's effectiveness, revise your total marketing program in those markets or look for your payout elsewhere.

2. *Spend when your timing is favorable.* When and if the carefully thought out strategy you've devised permits your agency to come up with great advertising copy, get the money out from under the mattress. You'll never regret it. As a matter of fact, set up a correlation between the quality of your advertising and your budget dollars. This will let your agency know exactly where its own profits come from. You'll be surprised at the results.

   Also, spend seasonally when the distribution of your sales by month suggests that. Then test a contraseasonal plan; it may work (although usually they do not).

3. *Consider how the life cycle of your product should affect your spending pattern.* On mature products, tend to spend in already successful areas. On new products, segment the daylights out of your market to pinpoint your best prospects. Then use brand development quantification (sales per thousand population in different market areas in which your product is sold as we showed in one of our sequential analysis exhibits) to help pinpoint where you're really *penetrating* markets. Then tend to go after that.

4. *Constantly market test your media plan versus new ones to improve your sales response curve.* The really smart advertiser puts 10% of his advertising budget aside for testing. It is the best advertising investment he ever makes. At the heart of the advertising spending problem, after all, is the fact that advertising is an activity the success of which is characterized by many variables. You just have to sort them out, and testing is the cheapest way.

In short, assuming you have your target market and advertising strategy straight, it pays to analyze your advertising spending. It still won't produce scientific answers. But it will produce *better* ones.

EIGHT

WILL YOUR

New Campaign
Really Sell?

Other than a decision on strategy, the biggest single commitment your company will ever make in advertising is to approve an ad campaign that executes it.

Now, in spite of the millions of words that have been written about what constitutes good advertising, knowing whether you have it is not all that difficult. Unfortunately, the creative side of advertising, and the copy approval process that goes with it, tends to bring out the best—and the worst—in all of us.

When all is said and done, the problem revolves around the fact that your company's advertising is designed to reflect *you*. And it's pretty hard to be objective about your innermost hopes, dreams, and aspirations when thousands, maybe even millions, of people are going to see them on display.

Keep in mind, however, that the creators of advertising are even less well known for being reasonable, fair-minded, objective people. It's up to you, therefore, to be a broad-minded critic of your advertising, rather than a mere tinkerer.

Copy approval is the *last chance* you have to confer the status of an investment on your advertising.

The key, therefore, is to have a well-defined set of standards for determining what you will or will not accept in the advertising that is submitted to you. What's more, if you adopt such a set of standards, I believe your agency will love you for it. For you will then provide an objective "check and balance" on their efforts which, if they're honest, they know they can't provide themselves.

At the risk of sounding dogmatic in an area where there are no infallible formulas, here is such a set of standards to think about.

GET TO THE ISSUE IN A "FLICK OF AN EYELASH"

It really is a busy, ad-saturated world, with lots of tougher customers out there than ever before. That's why it pays to look at every ad your agency ever develops—newspaper, magazine, television commercial, whatever—as if it's a roadside billboard you're driving past at 60 miles an hour. Because that's one way of telling whether it gets to your strategic story *fast*.

For apart from the fact that we live with ads all around us, consider that in advertising, you typically have to tell your story on one sheet of paper or less; within 60 seconds or less; or literally, on a billboard. Just to be noticed, in other words, every ad you run has to be a forceful distillation of your strategy that provokes its initial interest on the basis of a favorable image judgment.

What's more, there are two important corollaries to this. First, with strategy and brevity so paramount, your headline really is 90% of the battle in advertising. It is the "thinking man's" part of your ad that your readers, listeners, or viewers will see first, listen to first, and—you hope—take away in large numbers. That's why it's smart to limit yourself to one idea per headline. One idea per ad, in fact. Not because people aren't smart enough to get more than one. Rather, they just haven't the *time*. Oddly enough, this doesn't mean that short headlines are better than long headlines, or brief copy better than extended copy. The reverse may even be the case. The trick is not to overload 'em with *ideas*. One good one will do nicely.

Second, your illustration must work hand in hand with your headline to *dramatize* your story. What I mean here is this. Art exists not only to delight, but to instruct. To illustrate thought. And the art that illustrates the strategic idea you've worked so hard to develop, ought to be so good at dramatizing your selling message that it might actually tell your story even if unaccompanied by copy. The reverse of this, of course, is the "Art Director's triumph." The ad that is beautiful, faddish, up-to-date, an award winner. But which in terms of the all-important issue you're raising, signifies nothing.

Before closing on this point, it's worth mentioning that there is another important benefit to be had by insisting on simple ads, and simple headlines especially. Such ads tend to "write themselves." That is, because they concentrate on one powerful idea, your copywriter invariably finds it easier to develop his body copy in a forceful and convincing way. What follows the startling presentation of one clear and worthwhile selling idea, therefore, is the compelling development of it.

THE BEST WAY TO CONVINCE PEOPLE IS REASONABLY

There is a long-standing belief among agency people, and clients too, that advertising has to be emotionally charged-up to sell. It's as if they believe every ad should spill out with the type of wild evangelism that used to be projected in old-fashioned salesmen's "pep rallies."

Anyone who argues that advertising should not have an

emotional quality should, of course, have his head examined. But what I, for one, believe an ad should do is touch the emotions, not shatter them. The problem with emotionally over-sexed ads, in fact, is that they *don't* sell. And the reason they don't is simple. Unreality doesn't sell.

The ad that tries to hit the reader square on his nerve ends has a nasty way of picking up excess baggage too. Almost inevitably, they deal in cliche. But cliché is the antithesis of the fresh, relevant thought that gives the prospect's mind a good airing—and sets him on the road to changing his behavior because his perceptions and beliefs have been shaken. Overstatement creeps into such ads as well. But in the second half of the 1970s, if anything is out of style, it's pompous untruth. Today, the natural in advertising is in; the ad that looks like a double-knit suit is out.

Attention to this point—through careful review of the logic and believability of your ads—is one of the most important ways you can contribute to their improvement, therefore. The very *best* place to look for a passionate but reasoned tone to your ads, of course, is in the claims they make and the proof they offer.

For example, an ad that says

PALMOLIVE SOAP IS PREFERRED BY
2% MORE WOMEN THAN GENTLE CAMAY

is infinitely more believable than

PALMOLIVE WINS LATEST SOAP TEST!
SMASHES ALL PREFERENCE RECORDS!

no matter how clamorous and exciting the latter seems.

So next time you're presented with a new campaign by your ad agency, look for the benefits, testimonials, case histories, guaranties, demonstrations, and ingredients that are realistic. The body copy that is specific and concrete. The test you barely win. The admission, even, of some imperfection.

Consumers will *believe* you for it. And it will sell better because you've given useful information, not a lot of hot air.

THERE *IS* NO PUBLIC. ONLY PEOPLE

A third principle it pays to remember when your agency is showing you a new campaign, in that there are a great many people out there who are ready, willing, and able to be convinced by your ads. What you must do, however, is convince them one-by-one.

The trouble with most really bad ads, in fact, is that they are written to audiences rather than individuals. There is no milk of human kindness in them. As a result, they are "brag and boast" affairs that talk to a mindless (and unresponsive) mass.

Fortunately, when and if your agency starts presenting you this kind of stuff, your remedy usually is simple. Almost certainly your agency doesn't know enough about your customer. This is the time to get them out of that stale Madison Avenue air, talking to real people. And the key thing you should draw their attention to during this exercise is your customer's *life situation*.

How, for example, does a housewife, who washes a quarter million dishes in her lifetime, *really* feel about dishwashing detergents, including yours? Or how does the manager of a steel service center buying thousands of tons of flat-rolled per month *really* go about adding another vendor to his list?

To personalize your ads to the mentality and the vernacular of your prospects—to write ads that really get under a person's skin—you normally have a great ally in this educational process, your salesmen. For while you can get along with salesmen who don't appreciate the value of your advertising, you absolutely should not tolerate advertising men who have nothing to learn from your sales reps.

Advertising *is* selling after all. It's just that advertising people, and especially agency people, don't get sufficient opportunity to meet prospects face-to-face. Suggest that they do. Throw away the demographics and insist that they do. For "riding with the salesmen" will awaken real ad makers better than anything else to how your market really operates, why your product actually sells, and even whether their advertising is really working.

This approach should make your future advertising a lot more productive. Because if you talk to me as a person in your ads, I'll listen. But if you lecture me as an audience, you and your perfectly thought-out strategy can go fly a kite.

Some Ads that
Meet Our Criteria

You told her 7:00 sharp, Harry.
Where are you?

Obviously, Harry doesn't have an Accutron® tuning fork watch.

So he isn't guaranteed the right time to within a minute a month, without any winding.

And he's going to spend the rest of the night regretting it.

FOR MEN: #25532. 14K solid gold case. $500.

FOR WOMEN: #25906. Adjustable tapered bracelet. $135.

BULOVA ACCUTRON

*Timekeeping will be adjusted to this tolerance, if necessary, if returned to Accutron dealer from whom purchased within one year from date of purchase. ©Bulova Watch Co., Inc.

102

AN AD WITH REAL
BILLBOARD QUALITIES

WHETHER YOU'RE FOR
OR AGAINST GUNS,
THIS AD TELLS YOU A LOT ABOUT
THE BEST OF THEM

106

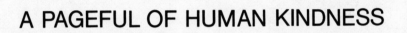

A PAGEFUL OF HUMAN KINDNESS

Some Ads
that Don't Meet
Our Criteria

SYMBIOTIC
(sĭm′bī·ot′ĭk)

SYMBIOTIC (sĭm′bī·ot′ĭk), adj. – an association of two
dissimilar entities from which mutual benefit is derived.

THE RHINOCEROUS AND THE TICK BIRD

Tick birds gain nourishment by eating the insects which live
on the rhino′s skin. The hostile rhino passively accepts the
birds′ presence for the rhino himself cannot remove the
annoying insects.

We like to think of our relationship with our pipeline customers as SYMBIOTIC — mutually beneficial.

OUR BRUSH LINE FOR YOUR PIPELINES

Milwaukee Pipeline Brushes are designed specifically for
pipeliners. We have the correct brush for each of the clean-
ing or welding applications in the yard or on the spread.

Our network of pipeline, welding and industrial distributors
backed up by our extensive factory inventory assure you
of immediate delivery.

110

SORRY, I DON'T NEED
A RHINOCEROUS TODAY

PROBABLY AN EARLY EFFORT
IN A NEW CAMPAIGN.
HOWEVER, IT FAILS TO PRESENT
A SINGLEMINDED STRATEGIC IDEA
IN A LOGICAL WAY.

TALKING TO YOURSELF.
A BAD MISTAKE

NINE

HOW P & G DOES IT

In every single year since the end of World War II, the biggest single advertising budget spent in the United States has belonged to the Procter & Gamble Company. Which has gotten a maximum return from its investment. A 300 million dollar company in 1945, P & G is a 6 billion dollar company today. Profits have multipled 17 times over the same period.

Moreover, one major competitior, no less formidable an advertiser than the Colgate-Palmolive Company, has recently acknowledged P & G's U.S. packaged goods leadership by "leaving the field" as far as its primary, future growth strategy is concerned. Like IBM in computers and General Motors in automobiles, P & G has spread-eagled its industry. And it has done it all through consumer advertising.

The interesting question is, "How?"

Is the air somehow more conducive to good advertising thinking 500 miles from Madison Avenue? Is there a guiding genius calling the shots for the company? Do they just make a better bar of soap or roll of bathroom tissue or tube of toothpaste, then simply let their advertising say so?

Well, there are elements of truth in all those things, because P & G has actually made physical distance from their advertising agencies into a virtue; have grown whole cadres of management excellence if not geniuses; and have consistently product innovated to provide the consumer with maximum

117

value, their copyrwiters with a maximum verbal toehold, and their brands with a maximum profitable life cycle.

Yet these things do not get to the core of P & G's success. Rather, the P & G secret is a unique, even an unremitting emphasis on individual brand advertising strategy; plus a test market process, aimed at quantifying advertising's results, that just won't quit.

ADVERTISING AS AN INVESTMENT

From a management standpoint, the first thing that strikes you about the P & G approach is the universality of the product manager. Not only does every brand have one (because P & G *is* one of those companies that must diagnose the wants of many markets), but it is the system they invented, and have stuck by lo these many profitable years, as sales and profits have marched relentlessly upward by 10% or more per annum.

What imitators of P & G have not always understood, however, is that the product manager is the creator of strategy, and only rarely the executor of it. The job is far more staff than line. And those legions of dedicated young men, whose dissection of their brand's advertising impact goes on and on, are proof most of all that advertising, approached with full awareness of its risks, is truly a strategic process, nothing like *The Hucksters* at all.

The secret of P & G's success is best underlined, in fact, by observation of the product manager's most time-consuming duty: distilling his thoughts into exhaustive and strategy-laden memos. You might even argue, not too facetiously, that the memorandum is the real key to the P & G system. Product managers under P & G's "up or out" policy come and go. But the memo goes on.

To whom does this memo go, and what does it say?

It goes to the product manager's division manager who, with more or less organizational layering between him and the PM, is a senior manager who could invariably leave for the presidency of a hundred million dollar (or larger) corporation tomorrow. Invariably too, the memo results in intensive review of some major or minor aspect of brand strategy (either marketing, copy, media, promotion, or even research), which is why the entire process is so endlessly purposeful, and never degenerates into a massive paper shuffle.

In short, by emphasizing an ethic of large-minded strategic thinking based on intensive review of the facts; getting the best young men available to do the "dog work"; then passing the detailed results up to senior management* for balanced decision making, P & G has raised advertising strategy to a high art.

First-rate strategic thinking is a necessity at P & G, of course, because the company's primary objective is *control* of its markets, as expressed in market share.† That is, P & G could never carve up its markets with multiple products the way it does (6 heavy duty detergents, 3 all purpose cleaners, 3 dishwashing lotions) without careful chartering of its brands in such a way that they compete more with the competition than each other.

Heavy emphasis on fact-based strategy also keeps P & G from pushing *too* hard for market share, or from rushing into a market. There have, for example, been very few new product mistakes at P & G. They recall TEEL fondly for this reason. It proves they're human, even if the real problem was faulty World War II ingredients that turned consumers' teeth black.

For a P & G agency not to join them in this insatiable thirst for strategic thinking is, of course, inadmissable. Invariably the gentleman with his agency personnel, the P & G executive nonetheless excels at the annual "blood brother" budget meeting when client and agency agree to rise or fall together.

These meetings—like the memos—are almost totally

* Many times those memos go right up to the sacrosanct "sixteenth floor."

† The inherent quality and consistency of its earnings are second, and earnings growth third.

strategic. Only if there is a serious question in everyone's mind about the degree of difficulty involved in executing a proposed course of action, is an executional question asked. A confident answer, frequently without elaboration, will generally suffice to gain approval. Blood brothers operate on trust—and performance.

Agency account executives have been known to faint during these meetings.

Agency account executives have been known to faint at the amount of work P & G demands from them too. Particularly in the anticipatory test marketing of alternative strategies throughout the company's numerous sales districts, till every last drop of truth or falsehood or profit potential is ground out of them. If advertising is an activity the success of which is characterized by many variables, P & G wants a quantification of them all.

Koyck's Model and the calculus get a scant hearing in such activity, however. P & G wants its testing done in real life. Which means nose counting "in the market."

And herein lies the second great strength of this company. If they are wrong in their approach to advertising a product, or if there simply is a better way, they find out fast and factually, then adapt. Humility is a virtue closely related to expediency in Cincinnati.

P & G even likes to be *proved* wrong by its agencies, particularly when it comes to spending too little money. Indeed, the best way to become a hero with them is to prove they're not spending enough on your brand. They know their agencies generally have the experience to buy extra media wth consummate skill (and they own the most efficient daytime TV shows anyway), so it's the correlation of payout business with significantly higher advertising spending levels that they really yearn for.

They have the boldness, in short, to spend on the basis of large strategic opportunity; on the basis of advertising as an investment.

Which brings up the question, can P & G be beaten? Sure. Every day. But (though they would say this is euphoric) really

only on the creativity of their copy, which is after all, not completely under their control.

Morever, when the White Knight or the All or the Janitor
In A Drum comes along, their incredibly quick response for
so large a company gets a line on their adversary fast. Where
they're being hurt, how much, at what rate, what to do about
it. How the memos fly!

That's when P & G adds creative imagination to strategic
thoroughness too. When the "dumb soap commercial" they
too frequently run in product mid-life gets yanked for something better. As good, frequently, as the copy they were smart
enough to run in introducing the brand.

All of which I believe holds a message for you, whether
your ad budget is 30 thousand, 3 million or, like P & G, 300
million dollars. Which is, in the high payout advertiser's operation, *structure, people, management philosophy, and strategic
processes all work together to a fare-thee-well.*

TEN

THE DILEMMA OF THE

Industrial Advertiser

There is a general feeling on Madison Avenue that consumer advertising is a faster track than industrial advertising. It is a feeling that doesn't hold water. For one thing, it is even harder in advertising industrial products to market test, measure the results of your advertising, or construct a media plan in which you have real confidence. The problem is that there are normally fewer customers to test against and fewer sales districts in which to test; advertising is typically a more integrated part of the industrial company's total marketing mix; and observance of the message weight or "voice level" principle isn't applicable in the industrial field, where far less media research exists.

What's more, virtually every industrial ad is an "institutional" ad. With far greater consistency, therefore, the industrial products company puts its very name and reputation on the line when it advertises. Many consumers don't even know who makes their cake mix or dishwashing detergent; but try selling most industrial products without letting your corporate-character "hang out" to provide believability to your sale.

And finally, there frequently is a more complex set of strategic factors to consider in mounting and executing an industrial advertising program. That's because the strategy development process in industrial advertising tends to be less well illumined by quantified data; and because nonmarketing considerations (such as high fixed-cost asset bases that must be kept operating) are generally more controlling in industrial company thinking.

All of which—less assurance in what you propose to do in advertising before you do it, greater downside as well as upside risk per ad, and greater complexity in developing and executing firm promotional strategy—tends as I say to make industrial advertising no picnic.

Recognizing this, what should the industrial advertiser do? Well, in keeping with the emphasis in this book on getting a payout from your advertising by approaching it strategically, here are some approaches you may want to consider.

IDENTIFY "THE MISSING LINK" IN YOUR MARKETING PROGRAM

While it is certainly true that inflation keeps business publication advertising costs escalating about as fast as TV or radio or other high cost consumer media, it also costs the average industrial products company the better part of a hundred dollars today just to have a salesman shake hands with a prospect. And at this cost level consistent direct sales coverage of the many decision makers, influencers, and brand specifiers who affect the sale of industrial products starts getting ridiculous.

More than ever, therefore, the role of the industral products salesman—the very nature of the job you want him to do—needs to be carefully spelled out versus the job you want advertising to do. Or, in other words, a "link" between the essential tasks of the *two* critical promotional tools in industrial marketing needs to be made if a company is to achieve total selling efficiency.

Industrial marketers often forget this point, concentrating on purely functional improvements in sales (compensation systems, territorialization, job coaching, etc.) and advertising (budgeting, media schedules, backing up sales with promotional materials) without really bringing these two marketing tools together as part of a "whole job."

In this respect, experience suggests that an industrial product salesman generally plays a cost efficient role for you if he concentrates on being a "closer," a negotiator of specifications, and a customer inventory consultant. By contrast, advertising's most productive roles in industrial marketing tend to lie in identifying new customers, disseminating product news, and demonstrating the potential impact of your product's features and benefits on your customers.

We have already advanced sequential analysis as one way of defining such roles, of course. But if nature has afflicted industrial advertisers with special problems in developing and executing their ad progams, it has provided at least one big compensating advantage as well. That is, while the customer himself is frequently "the missing link" in consumer advertising (since he is typically so numerous), in industrial marketing you can often go out and talk to half your volume in a week.

Even if the quantified evidence of your sequential analysis appears to tell you exactly what roles both sales and advertising should be playing, therefore, it makes sense to personally sniff around in the market too. Or better yet, have your salesmen do it *consistently*, since an in-depth knowledge of the profit potential, service needs, and merchandising approach of each and every one of your customers is a sine qua non of effective sales management anyway.

RUN CAMPAIGNS, NOT ADS

Procter & Gamble is not the only place where you frequently hear the phrase "advertising as an investment." It's often used in the industrial field also. The problem is, with too many industrial advertisers it is meant in a throwaway sense. "I'll run a couple of ads as an investment." As a hope, a dream that those ads will somehow, someday, produce some business, or at least ward off the evil spirit of sales decline.

The only thing this attitude ever really produces, however, is a little income for the advertising agency that doesn't have the wherewithal to turn down a fast buck. "Running a few ads as an investment" is like betting long shots at the racetrack, in other words. Rather, according to both experience and Morrill, it takes a *minimum* of a half-dozen ads in any one publication before you really make an impact.*

This should come as no surprise. Advertising is, after all, primarily a matter of credibility. And people in any walk of life who buy anything, don't believe you, and are unwilling to be led by you, until they get to know you. Advertising builds business all right; but a "couple of ads" are just claims from a casual acquaintance.

More than advertising measurements may ever tell us, that is, people buy from a company just because they remember and like it. In fact, the advertising world is full of products that are successful not because their customers are convinced they are superior, but just because their customers have come to know and feel comfortable with their makers.

Especially if your budget is limited, therefore, it pays in industrial advertising to spend on a "building block" basis, making sure you have adequate schedules in at least the leadership publications in your field. The publications with something to say, that is—about industry standards, trends, and controversial issues. The books with guts and brains.

Incidentally, these leadership publications are also

_____
* A positive impact, that is. A negative impact can be created in a single ad.

identifiable in that they are the ones that are balancing their circulation to include both vertical (management layer) and horizontal (functional specialist) readership. This is an especially attractive development for the smaller advertiser, because it permits him to put his reputation and capabilities versus those of his larger brethren "on the line" in front of his whole bloody industry.

WHEN FACED WITH IMPERFECT DATA IN CONSTRUCTING ADVERTISING STRATEGY, LOOK HARD AT YOUR BUSINESS SYSTEM

Looked at broadly, the information needed in advertising strategy development tends to fall into four general classifications: information on product movement from manufacturer to user; consumer usage and attitudes about the product; the post-measurement of advertising's effectiveness; and economic data. In every one of these categories, however, the industrial advertiser tends to have less to "go on" than his consumer goods counterpart. For example:

- Less data on product movement out to users (since warehouse withdrawal figures are rarely available in industrial marketing) means less knowledge about the condition of the inventory pipeline and, therefore, optimum advertising timing.
- Less knowledge about end-user attitudes and buying intentions (except that gleaned from current customers), means greater difficulty in allocating advertising spending across product, geographic, and distribution lines.
- And less knowledge about what has actually worked in advertising (according to data like Nielsen movement reports by sales district, or broad-based awareness studies) means a "harder go" in evaluating the realism of alternative strategies.

The industrial advertiser often has a number of serious information gaps to fill in constructing his advertising strategy, therefore. And while these gaps aren't serious enough to invalidate the fact-based approach to strategy we have been recommending, they should be compensated for if at all possible.

Now, in this respect, our chapter on profit economics dealt at some length with the subject of value added. An analytical approach designed to help the advertiser better understand his role in the marketing process of his industry, by understanding the economic relationship between *stages* in his industry.

With information about "what's really going on" in the typical industrial market harder to come by, however, "stage" information (which is acquired through personal industry contacts of the type we recommended a few pages back, rather than quantified research) takes an even greater importance. It therefore makes sense in developing industrial advertising strategy* to try to formulate as much *conceptual* marketing thinking about the stages in your industry as you can, building on the economic information of the same type you developed earlier.

That is, after "flowing out" the stages in your particular industry in this fashion:

Raw material———Manufacturers____ Wholesale ——End-use
sources   distribution   customers
                                           channels

it frequently is a powerful aide to the advertiser if he can come to grips with "big perspective" questions like the following:

• How is each stage in our industry structured? Who are the

* It makes sense in consumer marketing too. I just think the process has its maximum applicability in the industrial field, where a greater number of assumptions have to be made.

really important contestants in each, and what basic roles do they play in satisfying the end-users' ultimate needs?

- Who really controls the raw materials that go into our products? And if we did, could we make and market a significantly better product?

- What kind of competitors do we face, and how do our technical, service, and product development resources match up versus the best of them? Also, what is the capacity of each competitor, and what would be their likely response if our promotional programs began emphasizing an increased volume level or a different product mix or a higher price structure?

- What distribution channels does volume take as it flows out to the end-user? What geographic areas do various types of distributors cover, *how big is the volume flow through each channel*, and what kind of cost, margin, and service levels do different kinds of distribution deal in, compared to our distribution system?

Now, it doesn't take long to figure out that some of these questions would themselves be well served if supplied with quantitative answers. But the important thing is, they don't have to be, or the data fed into them can be "ballpark" without invalidating the strategic hypothesis you draw from them. And while a laundry list of questions about how your business system works will not neecssarily shed light on the specific informational "holes" you'd like to fill in constructing your ad strategy, it *will* give you a more precise notion of where key industry cost, competitive, and distribution factors can either constrain you strategically, or work greatly to your promotional advantage.

THE PRESIDENT MUST BE THE REAL LEADER IN ADVERTISING STRATEGY

We have talked at sufficient length in previous chapters about the nature of organizational commitment to advertising, to not have to repeat it all here. It's worth mentioning, however, that the heart of the problem in *executing* industrial advertising strategy is the greater potential for executive conflict that is "built-into" the average industrial product company. Not because such firms are inherently more political than their consumer goods counterparts, but simply because industrial company profits tend to be more subject to nonmarketing considerations. That is, things like utilization rates, degree of difficulty in manufacturing certain products, inspection standards, length of production runs, inventory policies and the like.

While industrial ad men tend to stump for selling features like short runs, custom components, and tight quality control, therefore, their counterparts in manufacturing, engineering, and finance typically favor (and are often paid for achieving), objectives like long runs, standardization of parts, and looser grading systems. With the result that unless goodwill or presidential leadership resolves these contradictions, a company can easily be on dangerous ground as to the *truthfulness* of its advertising claims.

Thus, while the industrial company president obviously does not assume personal control of his firm's ad program, he does have a special responsibility for seeing that his firm's advertising strategy is geared to both promotional *and* operational reality. For, just as advertising strategy development isn't easy, neither is the coordination needed to bring together the facilities, materials, quality controls, technical development programs, money, and people to deliver truthfully on advertising promises.

ELEVEN

ARE YOU A
Neglected Client?

More often than not, the advertiser who suffers from a lack of confidence in his advertising suffers from a lack of confidence in his agency. The principal emotion being a vague feeling of neglect. Unable to quite pinpoint the shortcomings in the service he's getting, however, client feelings often remain hidden in simmering resentment, thereby eating away at the mutual trust that is an absolute prerequisite to a productive client/agency relationship.

With the ante in advertising constantly rising, how can a client selecting an agency know beforehand what he's getting into? And, once in, what can he do to fix a relationship not completely to his liking?

In general, advertisers have found there are three main approaches that help solve these problems. Three *real* solutions that keep them from becoming second-class citizens, and conduce to advertising as a long-term success, rather than a short-term joyride.

The first is to look deeply into your agency's own objectives before hiring them. The second is not to be overawed by your agency. To *insist* on a definition of the "full service" you are promised at new business time and the delivery of that service later on, primarily through staffing by competent people. The third is to be a good client.

YOUR AGENCY'S OBJECTIVES

We agreed earlier that you will never communicate the ideals and standards of your firm unless you first define them; and unless you also project your product's real character rather than some trumped up "image" in your advertising, over the long term you are not likely to make much money from it.

If in light of this you infer that your own objectives and strategies are the only ones critical to the success of your advertising, however, you're wrong. For subtly, your agency's hopes, dreams, and plans have at least as much impact on the long-term results you achieve.

Few clients, for example, would disagree that there is no special virtue in working with an agency whose primary objective is to be "one of the biggest on Madison Avenue"; while one that aspires "to add a beer and a soap account next year" has an objective with no relevance to the advertiser's interests at all. Even an agency that just wants to "grow at a 15% compound annual rate to attract and motivate superior people" should probably be approached with scepticism.

What I am suggesting here is this. To fulfill their fundamental role as a professional service operation there is only one objective of meaning to the advertiser that an agency *can* aspire to: namely, constantly increasing marketing and advertising skill placed against problems of growing scope and complexity. Put another way, client service alone guarantees agency growth (as any wise, old, rich ad man will tell you). The stewardship of such large blocks of investment capital—which under the wrong advertising strategies can so easily be money down the drain—will have it no other way.

Now an agency that cannot make money for itself cannot be expected to make money for you either. But the paradox of an excellent advertising firm (like an excellent management consulting firm) is that it really is the exception to the rule that every business needs a business plan. It needs only a man-power development plan and adherence to professional goals in a commercial world.

Of course, if all this seems too, too high-minded in light of your personal experience with agencies, ask yourself on the other hand what kind of objectives P & G or General Mills or R.J. Reynolds look for in their agents' operations. And whether *you* will ever really be happy until you have people of this calibre working for you too.

TRUE FULL SERVICE

What percentage of agency new business presentations are made by Chairmen, Presidents, Copy Chiefs, and other as-sorted agency brass? Eighty percent? Ninety? Ninety-five?

Were I an advertiser reviewing agencies who wanted my business, however, I would insist they place their presentations almost entirely in the hands of the people who would later run my advertising. Getting a square deal from your agency, after all, primarily involves getting the day-to-day handling your expenditures warrant. Knowing the names of the senior agency executives who will "bail out" your account when it gets into trouble can only be of secondary concern, therefore. What you really need to know is the quality of the worker bees who will create profits for you from day one.

It's up to you, in other words, to ensure that you get more than a pack of sweet nothings from the agencies you interview at new business time. Infallible creative formulas that are paraded by the score; supposedly searching client question-naires that are answered as passionately (and ephemerially) as a love letter; and speculative presentations that are devel-oped on the basis of little more than educated guess, rather than on a knowledge of the economic role and profit sources that advertising can really exploit in your business.

If you're wise, you'll replace all these with a single-minded emphasis on getting top people from your agency. People who know how to join fact gathering and problem solving to creativity; who *are* good creators because they are first and foremost good thinkers; and people with the practical imagination and taste necessary to enter the culture of your audience, too.*

What's more, staffing with agency people who have both the talent and technique to approach advertising strategically, means they'll be less likely to knuckle under to you. That's because they'll have a sense of pride and assurance in what they do that will be reflected in straight talk and a willingness to be measured. They may even play the game the way it should be played. By being tougher with you than you are with them.

HOW TO TELL IF YOU'RE A GOOD CLIENT

In part because they *do* look for the wrong things at new business time, many clients later feel that their agencies are dropouts as far as management system is concerned.

The agency people who have been "put out to pasture" on their account then reciprocate by acting as if all the thinking and analysis their client wants help with, is just "busywork"— gunk that fouls their motor.

Both parties are probably at fault in this kind of situation. Only one is really under pressure to solve it, however. You, the advertiser. Keep in mind it's your money and reputation that are at stake.

The way you manage an agency of any talent for best results once you have them, therefore, is the same way you climb out of the "black box" of advertising to begin with. By a canny dedication to a management by objectives system that gives purpose and conviction to your whole advertising effort.

---

* If I had a nickel, for instance, for every ad I have ever seen that was written in "New Yorkese" rather than the true language of the prospect, I would be a rich man. More to the point—you might be too.

For you will never spur—or constructively threaten—an advertising man (or anybody else for that matter) to full realization of his God-given talents unless you kiss a seat-of-the-pants management system goodbye, and replace it with a programmed one.

The history of advertising, in fact, is full of profitable 40-year relationships that are based as much on good management as on brilliant ads. Especially management with a sound and consistent vision of what they really want to say to the world, and credibly can. Thereby making their accounts "a gem" that the best men in any agency will actually fight to work on.

Because, you see, the biggest secret of all of payout advertising is that there are large numbers of enormously talented and dedicated advertising people out there who are waiting to be sold something just as eagerly as anyone else. But, as always, it must be a product with character, well defined and promoted. Systematic, fair-minded management fits that bill perfectly.

Glossary

Term	Definition	Example
Budget	Plan of financial inflows and outflows.	Triumph Trophy's trade advertising spending will be $250,000.
Company philosophy	The beliefs and values underlying a company's operations, that add up to the way things "get done" within it.	Triumph Trophy is committed to managing its business in an open and fair-minded way, with an "open door" to ideas contributed by employees and suppliers.
Corporate objective	The end toward which a company's effort is directed.	Displace Pro Trophies as the leading supplier of trophy and award products in the total U.S. market.
Goal	The quantification of objectives. They specify a desired result or level of activity at a future point in time and measure progress toward the achievement of objectives.	Reach a 12.5% market share, with an ROI of 19.5% and dollar profits of $350,000.
Management processes	Both the formal systems and informal procedures by which work is done and executive cooperation achieved in a firm.	Triumph's management will hold quarterly review meetings to evaluate performance variances from advertising plan goals.
Management style	The human climate and conditions under which a business is run. Can be ad hoc, personal, power, or systems-oriented in nature.	Triumph Trophy's management requires the development of detailed strategy statements prior to advertising plan approval.

Term	Definition	Example
Marketing concept	An approach to developing and executing marketing strategies that establishes marketing as "the lead function" in a business. Foregoes a purely volume or sales-minded orientation to the business by assigning specific planning responsibilities to both top and line management.	Top management's role in the planning process will include providing guidelines for asset commitment; defining which products and markets are fair game for development; evaluating and challenging the alternatives developed by line management; then ensuring management coordination in execution. Line management's role will consist of defining problems, identifying opportunities, then outlining alternative strategies for top management to consider.
Marketing objective	An extension of corporate objectives. Consistent with them but also consistent with market realities. Provides ends for the marketing function in particular to achieve.	In the coming fiscal year Triumph Trophy's direct mail program will reach all sporting goods dealers carrying trophy and award product lines.
Marketing plan	Strategic plan for the marketing activities of a business, division, or product line.	Triumph's marketing plan for the coming year will consist of the following elements: a sequential analysis; a set of marketing programs, including an advertising plan; and a budget including specification of performance and spending goals by period.

Term	Definition	Example
Mission/charter	A special calling or area of operations. A special grant of powers.	Provide trophy and award retailers with the fastest and most reliable delivery practices in the trophy industry.
Plan	Primarily a set of strategic decisions and programs to guide the management of a business toward their objectives. In final form it also includes resource allocations, budgeting and scheduling details related to the execution of the plan.	To realize Triumph Trophy's objective of displacing Pro Trophies as the leading supplier in the trophy field, Triumph will continue its emphasis on developing and promoting a broader range of sports trophies. Therefore 28 new trophies of this type will be scheduled for development this fiscal year.
Policy	Principles upon which a course of action is based.	All advertising claims regarding dealer service will be limited to our proven ability to perform.
Position review	The analytical part of a marketing plan, that aims at providing the planner with sufficient knowledge about his product to permit him to develop fact-based objectives and strategies.	Triumph Trophy's position review indicates that high advertising spending levels correlate with high market share levels.
Positioning	An "against" strategy. A strategy that relates your product's features or attributes to those of competion.	Triumph's product policy is to capitalize on Pro Trophy's styling deficiencies, including the extra packing weight (and freight costs) necessitated by their heavy insert panels.

Program

A syllabus of action. A coherent group of actions.

Consistent direct mail program offering 72-hour delivery performance on complete line.

Profit economics

The interrelationship of price, volume, mix, cost, and investment peculiar to a firm, that determines how it basically makes money.

Given its high variable and low fixed costs, Triumph Trophy's profits are highly price sensitive.

Sequential analysis

A successive analysis of the major profit contribution elements in a company's marketing system, with the objective of producing a logical flow of quantitative evidence to guide advertising strategy development.

A complete example of sequential analysis is provided in Chapter 5.

Strategy

A plan for achieving an objective. In marketing, such a plan includes target user groups, plus the product policies and key appeals that will be followed.

Primary reliance for reaching Triumph's objectives will be placed on its direct mail program; advertising and key account sales coverage will be used as backups to this main business-getting tool.

Index